Connecticut
LITERARY ANTHOLOGY 2024
Poetry and Prose from the Nutmeg State

Laura Garrity, Sharbari Ahmed, Beth Gibbs, Dana McSwain,
Krisina Giliberto, Laura Taylor White, David Capps,
Linda Strange, Elizabeth Hilts, Moriah Maresh, Jack Sheedy,
Nancy Manning, Elisabeth Kennedy,
Chelsea Dodds, Heidi St. Jean, Jess Rasling, Elisabeth Kennedy,
Bill Conlon, Dana J. Graef, Jeff Schwartz,
Ed Ahern, B. Fulton Jennes,
Steven Ostrowski,
Jen Payne,

Edited By
Victoria Buitron
Summer Tate
Christine Kandic Torres

Publication of this book is funded by an anonymous donor-advised fund at the Hartford Foundation for Public Giving. The editors and Woodhall Press are grateful for their support.

2024
Connecticut
LITERARY
ANTHOLOGY

Victoria Buitron
Christine Kandic Torres
Summer Tate

woodhall press

Woodhall Press | Norwalk, CT

woodhall press

Woodhall Press, Norwalk, CT 06855
WoodhallPress.com

Cover design: LJ Mucci
Layout artist: LJ Mucci

Library of Congress Cataloging-in-Publication Data available

ISBN 978-1-960456-29-8   (paper: alk paper)
ISBN 978-1-960456-30-4   (electronic)

First Edition
Distributed by Independent Publishers Group
(800) 888-4741

Printed in the United States of America

Table of Contents

Fiction

Nonfiction

Poetry

Fiction

Introduction

Let's not pretend here: I am new to the Nutmeg State. Along with several thousand other New Yorkers after the pandemic began, I decided to leave my hometown of Queens, New York, to move to coastal Connecticut to consolidate my family into one intergenerational household. (I negotiated with myself that I was still on the Long Island Sound; this was just a shift in perspective.) It has been an adjustment to rely on a car most days, to find good Szechuan, to learn which aisles at Stew Leonard's employ a mechanical stuffed animal cabaret act to distract my preschooler—but a fair trade by many accounts, to be able to work comfortably from home, to access hiking trails through the woods in under five minutes, and to meet wonderful local writers who have welcomed me and helped to expand my literary community throughout Fairfield County.

From a craft perspective, what I take from my time in New York City is a strong commitment to place, not only as setting but as character in my fiction. The stories in this year's anthology demonstrate that commitment to community in all its complexity as well: from a working-class school auditorium in Waterbury, to the power-hungry Foxtail Condo Homeowners Association; from the crack-haunted streets of Fair Haven, to the highly manicured lawns of Darien, to London, to the Vineyard, and beyond. So many tackle the question of home—that is, wanting to escape home; to control it; to protect, to renovate; even to seek unlikely refuge in an abandoned one. These short stories captured different, though perhaps uniquely Connecticut perspectives from across the state, and impressed me with their ability to endear, surprise, and compel the reader to evaluate their own role in our communities, families, social systems. These stories push the boundaries of taboo, test the limits of friendship and the bonds of marriage, and blur the lines of reality. And some just have really fun villains, too.

I hope you take your time to savor these eleven short stories from your fellow Nutmeggers—a moniker I can now say I am honored to share with you all.

Christine Kandic Torres

Aurora Lights

By Jessica Galán

The first time you see Karina Castro, you're painting your toenails on the front stoop when a puttering vehicle pulls up. Two figures stir inside the car for a few minutes before a woman wearing tight jeans and heels exits, opening her hatchback to mirrors, lamps, and trash bags. But you're eyeing the shadow lingering in the car. When a girl around your age emerges, your bottle of Wet & Wild slips. Skin and bones to her curves are what you are—and if someone were to scalpel your wrist, you'd surely bleed green.

"Corner unit went quick," your mother whispers behind the screen door. Billowing clouds move in from the west and rain pelts the crabgrass—not that the downpour slows this new chick down. You stare at her shapely legs crouching down for milk crates. Only when thunder cracks the sky do you grab your files and polish and shelter from the summer aguacero.

That evening, you find the new girl collapsing boxes. You try to feign indifference as you pass her.

"Hey," she says, "I'm Karina."

You make like you don't hear—side-eye her instead because project females are rivals first: ones who primp and preen hoping they'll become The Chosen Ones, who ride with older boys in bass-booming lowriders, doing things your mother would belt you for.

Walking home, you ponder her confidence, confused a little by her warm smile. You come to an abrupt halt when you notice slivers of green erupting through the seams of the pavement. You wonder if those new shoots are her doing. You wonder if Karina brought the rain.

Ruthie's waiting at the back steps. "Karina's mother went to school with mine," she says.

It marvels you, how fast your neighbor finds shit out. You need school to start already. You're almost grateful Ruthie dropped out because it's the only time you can escape her.

The following afternoon, you're about to walk to Eggy's for a sugar fix when Ma blocks you.

"Stay put—there's cops outside." Beyond the door, news reporters and cameramen abound.

"What's wrong?"

Ma raises her chin towards the rowhouse across the playground. "A boy went missing."

A sinking feeling blooms inside your gut because you know what strung-out monsters have the capacity for. You tell her that they'll find him, but you know it's probably already over.

You don't want to hear anymore and feel ancient as fuck sludging upstairs. Exhausted is what you are from the uptick of violence and police sirens. Just a few days earlier, an addict pulled you behind the tall shrubs of your house—a sinewy bastard who pushed his rough hand down the front of your shorts. You fought him off till he staggered away shouting gibberish at the sky. The memory of how his rotted teeth clinked against yours still lingers.

You slide down the back of your bedroom door and let the hot tears fall, not because you're sad, but because you're angry. You want more than crumpled reefer bags and empty crack vials—you need to find a way out of Fair Haven.

Karina strolls over uninvited a few days later with a confused look in her eyes. Search dogs and detectives comb the fields across the playground.

"I figured this place was safe," she says.

"It's safer inside."

She plops onto the sofa, looking around the living room. You're embarrassed of Ma's ever-growing knick-knack collection—dusty shit you're forced to Pledge Saturday mornings.

5

Karina grabs one of the fake roses from the vase. "Ever smelled a real one?"

You think of the musty orange flowers in front of the house on Saltonstall Ave. "Not really."

She twirls its plastic stem. "Smells like calm—like magic."

You snatch the rose out of her hand and dip your nose into it. "Magic that'll transport us the fuck out of here?"

Together you cackle deep . . . and now you want to know this girl forever.

They charged the missing boy's father with his death a week later. A search crew found his body inside a garbage bag beside Mill River.

"Dope fiends," your mother says, staring at the news wide-eyed. "If anyone ever offers—don't you dare."

"If you're so worried, let's move."

It's easy for her to dish out advice—like she's accomplished—but boxing dress shirts at Ann Taylor?

"With what money?"

"None of yours," you answer.

"Mal agradecida," she replies, voice cracking.

You storm upstairs and shut the bathroom door. Run the water to drown out her continued yelling from downstairs. Drop your behind on the ledge of the bathtub. You're on her side for always, not that you'll ever tell her that.

Sometimes you can't help but feel like you want to pack your shit and leave. Three years back, Papi slipped into some blanca's car with New Jersey license plates. Gave you a single nod before he zoomed off. At fifteen, you believed your mother's version of what went down and let your anger for him grow like weeds. But when he wrote you a one-pager in little-boy pencil, you struggled with guilt. His misspelled words became your fuel for learning.

On the first day of school, Karina's dressed in the same blue t-shirt and white jeans from a few days ago. Without a bookbag or anything, so you hand her your extra notebook and two unsharpened pencils. She places an arm around your neck. "Promise to get you back, Flaca."

Only the warm glow of the overhead projector illuminates the shade-drawn science room. A teacher you've never seen before places a transparency over the heated glass. The bare wall becomes undulating waves of purple and green. Against the night stars, those vibrant swirls of color trident your soul. You place your binder over your chest, afraid the others will hear your thumping heart. You turn to Karina, but she's in the corner with her head down, black curls cascading over her desk.

"Aurora borealis," the teacher enunciates. "Tiny, charged particles of light trapped inside the earth's magnetic field—any idea where they're found?"

"Russia?" you ask.

"Close," he replies.

"The North Pole," last year's know-it-all declares.

After the final bell, you weave through the crowd of students with Karina for the bus and rush home because stuffed inside your closet is an oversized *Atlas of the World*. You want to know how far you'll have to go to reach those lights.

Anytime you and Karina walk Grand Avenue, you're catcalled.

"So do you like it?"

"When guys whistle?"

"I meant school—Fair Haven."

"It's okay."

You stop at Eggy's for penny candy because Karina's desire for sugar is worse than yours.

"At this rate, I'll be wearing dentures soon," she says.

Outside, you notice Watusi, an up-and-coming dealer, gazing intently from his Cadillac. You watch how he twirls a toothpick from his perfect pillowy lips. You try making eye contact, but he's staring at Karina instead.

"I'm crossing."

Karina digs her heels into the sidewalk and pulls your arm back. "Why?"

Watusi trails behind in his car. "What's in the bag?" he calls out.

Karina ignores him—teethes her Sixlets seductively.

"I got better dulce," he chides. He trails you to the playground bench as both of you suppress giggles.

"Ain't y'all kinda old for the park?" he asks.

"You know a better place to play?" she boldly replies.

"I do," he says, "but come for a ride."

She looks into your eyes. "Should I?"

"He sells—are you dumb?"

Her eyes narrow. "At least I'm not a prude."

Karina rises from the bench—like a moth to light, sauntering towards his car. It's too far to pick up their exchange, but the high note of her laughter burns your insides. She slides into his car and he peels away from the curb without a goodbye. Walking home, you curse your newfound friend's existence, wishing she had never stepped foot in Fair Haven.

She shows up a week later, love bites peppering her neck—Watusi's way of claiming her, you figure.

She reaches for your arm, squeezing it gently. "Sorry I haven't been around."

You yank your arm away. "I get it—we're not girls anymore."

Karina dumps the contents of her purse onto your bedspread. Between her keys, lipstick, and breath mints you notice a condom.

"Did you do it?"

"Yeah."

"Did it hurt?"

8

"A good pinch," she moans playfully.

"Fucking puerca!"

She puts on a black nightgown, clasps her breasts. "He loves these tetas," she says, eying her profile in the mirror. "Let's see yours."

You gulp back saliva. "No, weirdo."

"How am I gonna help you get play?"

You relent—unhooking your bra to nipples and chest bones. Karina laughs.

"You need help in the titty department."

Your face heats red and you reach for your flannel pajamas. "Fuck off, at least I'm still a virgin."

"Keep it that way," Karina says, turning off the lamp and pressing her spine to yours.

Late October and you're sitting in your guidance counselor's office. The walls are plastered with posters of collegiate buildings in faraway places.

You ask, "Is something wrong?"

"Not at all," she scans a manila file and invites you to sit. "These grades tell me you can handle college."

"What if I want to work full-time?"

"Southern's right over the bridge—did you know that?"

"I need to help my mom."

The counselor pushes applications towards you. "In the long run, a degree would, Nieves."

"Yeah, but you don't know what's happening around my way."

"I do, but—"

"Where do you live?"

"Guilford."

It's only twenty minutes away, but Guilford is manicured lawns and mansions, nuclear families, and wealth. That's all you need to hear.

On a Saturday in late January, you're rewriting science notes when small pebbles tap against your bedroom window. Outside, Karina's dressed in a new leather coat, giving you ballpark gestures as she points to Watusi's new ride. You signal with your hands to hold on.

"Watusi brought his boy," she says as both of you run towards the car.

You ride towards Mill River Park where the newly-poured sidewalks are crystalline against the lamp posts. A yellow moon hovers over the drawbridge.

You lean against the metal railing, trying to ignore the ice wind wrapping around your bare ankles. Chino stands beside you stinking of kitchen grease and cologne.

"You haven't spoken since the ride," you snap, ready to smack the smirk off his beyond-stoned mug.

Chino only yawns, plunks jagged rocks into the river below. "My old man got me a job at Campbell's."

"Soup cans, huh? Is that it?"

Chino's face drops. "Damn—you're foul."

"I'm getting me a house in Guilford. A baby."

He licks his lips, inches closer. "You need a man before a baby, right?"

"Not in Fair Haven, you don't."

Chino's laughter bouncing off the water eases you. He opens the lining of his jacket and gulps back his bottle of peach schnapps, handing it over to you after a long burp. It burns your throat yet loosens the fear you've carried since the incident in the bushes.

"Come June, I'm out."

"It ain't so bad," Chino replies.

"If you want to rot, then no—guess not."

Karina's yelps cut into your conversation. A few feet ahead, Watusi strips off her leather coat and dangles it over the railing.

"Say I won't," he challenges.

She pounds her fists on his chest, pleading for her coat back.

Watusi jumps onto a cement chess table, shouting into the night, "I motherfucking will."

In the moonlight, floating in the water, Karina's coat dances. You wait for it to sink, but it only flails its arms in the water, then glides over a small dip.

You follow Watusi, the four of you drunk, quiet ducklings stumbling towards his car.

You're silent the entire ride back, avoiding the roach clip they pass between them.

Back home, after showering, Karina pulls a comb through her wet hair. Greenish-purple sweeps across her bicep reminding you of the aurora lights.

"Do you like him?"

"I don't know."

"Chino's a top dealer—he's good for you."

Good like Watusi? you wanna say. You lock eyes with her reflection—point at her bruise. "From tonight?"

"You know how he is," she says, climbing under your covers.

She fades out easily, but you're fully awake, thinking about Watusi's New Year's Eve party. For a few seconds, he'd playfully trapped you at the top of his basement stairs. You turned away when he tried kissing you, not because you didn't want to, but because you knew better.

All winter, you make excuses when they come around and keep your distance until the April thaw. You're two weeks reunited with her when a girl brandishing a box cutter grabs Karina by the hair and straddles her to the ground. A blade catches her cheekbone, but you're frozen, unable to respond to Karina's cries. A crowd forms and you stay beside her until the paramedics carry her away.

You beep Chino, but he doesn't call until an hour after.

"Where's Watusi?"

"Busy, why?"

"They jumped Karina."

Silence on his end.

"Why didn't you tell her?"

He raises his voice. "About what?"

"That he has other girls."

"You're blaming that shit on me?" Chino says before hanging up.

Except for a woman pushing her child on the swings, the playground's empty. So, you feel like only half a fool climbing the log pole's wrap-around tires waiting to hear from Karina. When younger, you'd come here to escape flying daggers of unfamiliar Spanish your parents hurled back and forth. Now you're back, with a new ache clawing the inside of your ribs with your best friend maimed.

That evening, Karina's stone-faced mother opens the front door, hardly acknowledging you. Karina rests on a soiled, shabby couch. A gauze patch extends from her eyebrow to her jawline, her face puffy and sallow.

"Forty-eight stitches," she says. "Almost cut a nerve."

Karina's a small bird in your arms, smelling faintly of dried blood and medicine.

"Fuck him, Karina."

"He apologized—anyways, we're leaving."

"Why?"

Karina points a finger to the shuffling footsteps above. "She doesn't want me here."

"Stay with us."

She touches her bandaged face. "I can't."

"Where are you going?"

"Bridgeport."

It feels like a punch to your gut when she says it—Karina getting out of Fair Haven before you.

12

After graduation, you take a cashier job at Pathmark where your new boss keeps you at the register closest to his two-way mirror.

"Hermosa," his asp-tongue whispers, eyeing your new breasts when you ask him for your fifteen. With Karina gone, you filled out, eating in the loneliness and boredom: Export crackers slathered in butter, pork rinds, and bags of plátano chips.

Chino's in the parking lot when you clock out. Your grudge against him lingers still.

"What are you doing here?"

He shows you his car keys—points towards a spiffed-up Camaro. "Come for a ride."

He drives to Lighthouse Point, where you're both out long enough for lightning bugs to crash into you. Chino grabs your hand and pulls you towards the baseball field.

"Remember what you said last year?"

Between the house parties and late-night drives, you can't recall. "No."

"About the house . . . the baby?"

"What about it?"

"I want that, too."

Chino's not the man for you, but you give in to his awkward kiss. And when he slips a hand underneath your blouse, you imagine you're as beautiful as Karina.

Home by midnight. From the passenger window, you see the orange glow of your mother's cigarette tap against your doorstep. She puts it out, leaves the front door ajar. Chino flicks the foam dice hanging off his rearview. "She said you got promoted."

"Lead cashier—big shit."

"I thought you wanted college."

"What's that supposed to mean?"

"Nothing," he says.

He kisses your forehead and tucks a folded piece of paper into your palm.

On your day off work, you train to Bridgeport and trek towards 304 Grand Street—a brick three-family building, its gutters lined with discarded lottery tickets and broken glass. A place no different than your own. An older woman answers the first-floor doorbell.

"Is Karina around?"

"Who are you?"

"A friend from high school."

She eyes you up and down, deciding if she should answer.

"She just left. Come back in a few."

You round the corner for the convenience store and a woman appears before you.

Karina—hollowed out—reeking of sun-soaked garbage. When she registers who you are she slinks backwards, staccato-like in her shuffles, glancing at your gold wristwatch.

"Karina?"

She walks away from you.

"Come back with me."

A tinted-window car pulls beside her.

"No," she mutters, jumping into its back seat.

Crackhead. Basehead. Candy-eater. That's what they would've called her if she came home with you that day. Sorrow hits like an anvil as you walk towards the train station. An onslaught of buzzing cicadas heckle.

Training home, you think of your Karina. The one who showed you how to stuff your bra and flirt with boys. Who ordered takeout when your cupboards were empty. Faithful to you when Ruthie distanced herself. Your Karina waited on the steps most mornings with cups of café con leche for both of you, eyes bright against the world before all this shit went down.

14

Seven years have passed—not that you've left. It would've taken you over four thousand miles just to reach the northern lights, but you've hardly traveled.

You've made it to assistant manager, and when Ann Taylor pink-slipped dozens, you gave out jobs to countless people. The first rounds didn't affect your mother, but when they did—you watched her deteriorate from kidney failure, nursed her as best as you could until she passed.

You bought a condo facing the Quinnipiac River and ignored the Polish maintenance man who kept leaving potted flowers on your porch steps, but you caved when he tucked a single fragrant rose into your mailbox.

You're piecing together next week's schedule when Karina Castro casually strolls into your store. Adrenaline floods your veins as you watch her move between the aisles. Your hands tremble as you rise from your desk.

Karina's eyes go big when you block her shopping cart. "Nieves," she says.

No amount of powder can cover the silvery curl of her faded stitches; neither can her red lipstick deflect from her discolored teeth.

"I looked for you, Karina."

"I know," she replies.

"My mother died."

"Ruthie told me—I'm sorry."

She wears a thin gold band on her left hand.

"You've married?"

"Yeah," she says, eyes going damp, "I'm two years clean, too."

"That's good."

At the end of the aisle Chino lingers before offering you his sheepish grin. You smile, surprised by his head of pepper-gray hair. Karina leans against her husband, locked in solidarity.

"I made like those colorful lights were waiting for me."

15

"Lights?"

Confusion furrows your brow until you realize what she means—you never thought Karina had paid attention.

The Junkyard Madonna

By Laura Garrity

1.

The statue of the Madonna appeared out of nowhere overnight. She was made of car parts and other bits of assorted scrap metal, and in the center of her chest was a heart of amber glass that might have been a beer bottle in its previous life. Somehow, the artist had formed a veil of aluminum that suggested folds of fabric rippling in the breeze. Her head was crowned with roses made of what looked like chicken wire folded thick upon itself, and she stared down at Carl with a benevolent smile.

Carl almost walked right into her when he came out for his morning cigarette. She was big, probably seven feet tall. He spun around, looking for whoever might have left the thing, but with all the stacks of scrap and abandoned cars in the junkyard there were just too many places to hide. Carl looked back at the Madonna again. Every time he looked, it seemed, there was something else to notice in it. And though he wasn't much for art, or for church even, he was suitably impressed by the work that must have gone into something like that. He was so absorbed that he didn't hear Gloria walk up behind him.

"You forgot your coffee. I figured I'd . . ." she trailed off and stared, eyes wide and round. "Oh, heavens, what is that?"

"Well, I guess she's supposed to be Virgin Mary, with the veil and all."

"But—where did she come from?" Gloria asked, whispering so as not to offend the statue.

"Don't know. Was here this morning. Just found her now." Gloria crossed herself. "Do you think it's a sign?"

Carl snorted. "Sign we need to break down and get that security camera." Carl wasn't much for security either; the worst that ever happened was that the high school kids would sneak in every once in a while, and he'd have to clean up the butts and bottles. But if anyone had ever stolen from him, they'd never taken anything big enough for him to notice. "Wonder how they got it in here. Must have needed a truck to haul something that heavy, or a van at least. You'd think we'd wake up if someone backed a van into the yard in the middle of the night, wouldn't you?"

"It's beautiful, in a strange way, don't you think?"

"It's impressive, that's for sure."

After a cautious attempt at rocking the statue to gauge its weight, Carl decided to leave it where it was. It wasn't blocking the driveway, and he figured it was what his mother would have called a "conversation piece."

2.

Two weeks later the pilgrims started coming. Gloria had invited some of the ladies from church over to see the statue, and word had spread from there. The pilgrims were mostly older women who would quietly pray the rosary before the Madonna or reverently lay grocery store roses at her feet. Carl really didn't mind, although Gloria did feel some pressure to make the junkyard a little nicer, if all these ladies were going to be visiting.

Peter Shephard from Local 7 came by and interviewed them, but there really wasn't much to say. Peter Shephard didn't seem very impressed with Carl's version of the story, ("I came out for a smoke, and there she was,") but it was the simple truth after all.

They did air the story though, showing the statue in great detail, and Carl in quite less detail, playing up the mystery angle. *Then* the excitement started.

3.

The art crowd started arriving in droves, clogging up the parking lot and irritating the pilgrims. Young men with beards and heavy scarves tried to explain to Carl that his Madonna was "important work." They pointed to bits and pieces and tried to explain how this or that meant this statue was clearly *Yumo*.

"Yumo?" he asked. "Is that a person?"

A girl with sunglasses that made her eyes look like those of a giant insect waved her arms wildly.

"See?" she cried. "He chose you and you don't even know who he is!"

One of the bearded men nodded thoughtfully. "Exactly something Yumo would do."

Carl sighed. "So it *is* a person?"

"An artist," the girl confirmed. She sipped coffee gingerly from a mug with a pink flamingo for a handle. Gloria insisted on serving coffee to all the visitors, pilgrims and artists alike. "He's very mysterious. He just leaves things in public places, like here . . ."

"It's not exactly a public place though," Carl muttered under his breath.

"You should really get this to a museum," she continued. "Sometimes they just disappear overnight! People steal them, or maybe he just comes and takes them back . . ."

Carl didn't know of any art museums nearby.

"Maybe we should bring it to St. Gabriel's?" one of the pilgrims suggested timidly.

A man whose face was barely visible between his hat, scarf and beard scoffed. "A local church? This belongs in a major museum! You should call the Art Institute of Chicago—I bet they'll even come and get it for you."

At this idea the pilgrims let out shouts of protest.

"What if it's not even this Yumo's?" Carl asked. Two of the men looked at each other and rolled their eyes in unison.

"It's *definitely* Yumo," the woman drawled, and the others chattered in agreement.

4.

One afternoon, about a month after the Madonna's appearance, the art dealer appeared. The woman had knocked politely at the door, introduced herself as Madelyn Lender and asked to see the Madonna. She was dressed in an expensive-looking navy suit with her face made up, but wore sensible flat boots. Gloria brought her coffee, in the nicest mug they had: the Pfaltzgraff tea rose that wasn't chipped or stained yet. Madelyn held the coffee with the blissful expression of a child with cocoa on a cold day. She strolled around the statue, looking at it with clear appreciation.

"Do you think it belongs to this Yumo?" Gloria asked.

"I think it's very likely," Madelyn answered.

"Should it be in a museum?" Carl asked. "That's what all those art kids kept saying."

She considered, taking a sip of her coffee. "Well, that's a matter of philosophy, isn't it? If you're really asking if it's worth a lot of money, then yes, I should imagine I could get you quite a haul at a collector's auction. In a museum, it could be protected from theft and the elements. But is that really the best thing for her?" Madelyn gave an extravagant shrug.

"More people could see her then," Gloria said.

Madelyn smiled. "True. But would it be the same? There would be hundreds of pieces around her. Better and more important ones, mind you. Would the experience mean as much as it did for the people who had to make a journey to a junkyard in the middle of nowhere—beg your pardon—to see it?"

"Like pilgrims," Carl said quietly, watching the sun dance off the statue's steel robes.

Madelyn tilted her head to the side thoughtfully. "That's right," she nodded, "pilgrims. I like that, yes." She took out her phone. "Do you mind if I take some pictures?"

"Oh, go right ahead," Gloria offered.

Madelyn circled the statue and took one picture after another. Multiple angles, closeups, documenting the Madonna in her entirety. When she was done, she turned to them and gestured for them to move closer to the statue. To Carl's surprise, she took their picture standing in front of it.

"Oh, that's a good one, you're such a sweet couple."

Carl laughed and put his arm around Gloria. "Well, I've always thought so!"

Madelyn took a business card from her pocket and handed it to Gloria. "I can see you have a lot to think about, and there's no need to rush. Take some time to talk it over, and if you want to sell, give me a call. Or if you want to lend it to a museum, well, I can help you with that too."

Gloria tucked the card primly in her dress pocket. "We'll talk about it, thank you."

Carl walked Madelyn Lender across the lot to her car. "Thanks for coming out to see her," he said.

She reached out and shook his hand. "Thank you for letting me—and all those others too."

Carl froze and looked down at Madelyn's hand in his. It was a small hand, as he would expect from a woman of her size, but the feel . . . Most of Carl's customers were mechanics. Madelyn Lender's hand felt like the hands of those men, calloused and rough with work. His heart pounded in his ears.

She leaned closer and looked at him with concern. "Carl, is everything alright?"

21

"Tell me," he asked, "how did you get it here without us hearing you?"

She went still, then closed her eyes and tilted her face toward the sky. He stood patiently and waited. "In pieces," she finally admitted. "Five pieces, over the course of a week. That last night, I just assembled her."

He let out a deep sigh. "Of course. It didn't even occur to me."

"It wasn't exactly easy, you know. Even in pieces," she said over her shoulder as she got in the car.

"I won't tell anyone," he blurted out, "you know, that you're the Yumo."

She leaned out the open window and smiled at him. "I know," she said. And lifting her hand in a final wave she set off down the driveway, kicking up dust and gravel in her wake.

Barbarian

By Mackenzie Hurlbert

To kill time that summer, Barb picked through the shadows of Ghost House. Looming over the abandoned lot at the end of her block, the green Victorian's shattered front windows and caved-in porch reminded her of a slack-jawed corpse—not that Barb had really ever seen a dead body, but she'd watched a lot of *Law and Order* and got the gist. Local lore about the house was endless sleepover fodder, only to be whispered after all the lights were turned off: Ghost House had bodies buried in the basement, figures passing behind the upstairs windows, a child's laugh echoing through the halls. Barb considered it all goosebump-inducing fun.

Most kids at school hated Ghost House and double-timed their pace if they were forced to pass by. Her parents hated it because it "decreased the neighborhood's property value." Barb loved it, peeling paint and all.

After her parents went to work and the neighborhood kids rode their bikes to the lake, Barb crept through the thigh-high overgrowth of Ghost House's backyard and explored the cool shadows beyond the kitchen door. She was disappointed to learn she wasn't the first one to brave its halls—broken bottles and crumpled cigarette cartons littered the hardwood floors. The living room's wallpaper had been tagged red with "GHOST HOUSE," as if the label added truth to the legends.

Regardless, she preferred the solitude of Ghost House to her own home, where if she watched TV, she had to put up with her mom's porcelain clown collection gawking at her from the mantel. Their glittering eyes seemed to track her across the room—a sensation far creepier than anything she came across at Ghost House.

23

Ghost House was definitely better than the nearby lake, where her neighbor Tommy Legge often lurked with his crew of nose-picking idiots. Tommy had coined the nickname "Barbarian," creatively twisting Barb's full name into something that pointed to her size. She'd inherited her dad's height and shoulders, and while the doctor said she wasn't overweight, she was, as her mom would say, "big-boned." She stood taller than all the other kids in her grade, taller than most of the older kids and even some teachers. And thanks to her most recent growth spurts, she'd shed the beanpole shape of her girlhood and developed into something soft and unfamiliar. As if she wasn't taking up enough space already, Barb felt powerless as her hips widened and her chest grew heavy, curves appearing where there used to be straight lines.

"What a lovely young woman," her mom's friends often said, but Barb didn't want to be a woman, at least not yet. She walked through the world with a perpetual slump. Maybe if she'd been a basketball player or a boy, her height would have given her some advantage. But Barb was as athletic as a hedgehog and no matter how hard she tried, her height made her stand out. That was exactly what she didn't want—to be this freakish "young woman" in a sea of petite girls and mean boys.

Barb spent the first day in Ghost House sweeping up the glass and trash, her mother's voice droning in the back of her mind about tetanus risks. She then started exploring the closets, dressers, and attic for artifacts from when the house was a home: old suitcases, a slide projector, and newspaper clippings that crumbled between her fingers.

One day she found a stack of letters tucked in an ancient roll-top desk, the cursive script barely legible except for the opening line: "My Dear Friend." The words were a stomping boot in an abandoned room—stirring up her loneliness like clouds of dust. Her two best friends were away all summer; Alice at sleepaway camp and Sam with her aunts in Utah. She texted them daily, missing the comforting balance of them bracketing her like bookends.

Barb used Ghost House as a distraction from her loneliness and worked her way through each room of the first floor methodically. She then moved to the bedroom at the top of the stairs, where she spent the morning picking through a closet of Christmas decorations. Tinsel garlands and a rainbow wheel lamp. Ornaments as fragile as eggshells and nests of tangled lights.

Through the shattered window, she heard the tinkle of an ice cream truck weaving closer, block by block. She paused, listening to its siren call. Sweat gathered on Barb's upper lip and she wiped it away using the shoulder of her shirt, an oversized Harley Davidson tee she stole from her dad. It draped over her frame like a poncho, dwarfing her and making her feel a little less like a giant. She loved it, getting lost in its size.

The heat was brutal, and the shadows of Ghost House gave little to no relief. She shifted one box out of the way and opened another, untucking the dusty cardboard flaps and rifling through layers of newspapers to unveil stockings with names embroidered into each cuff.

"Bryan, Brandon, Brenda . . ." Barb lifted them up one at a time and laid them out on the dusty floor. She fished more newspaper out of the box, along with some gift bags and a handful of bows. There at the bottom was another stocking, rolled up and tucked in the corner. She pinched it just in case some unsuspecting mouse had nested within and gasped as it unfolded.

"Barbara." As her name left her lips, a breeze swept through the broken window and rustled the tinsel piled by her feet.

Something fluttered to the floor. She laid the stocking alongside the others and bent to retrieve a two-dollar bill. Unfolding the money, she laid it carefully across the stocking with her name.

Down the hall, a door slammed. Barb froze. *Was someone in the house?*

"Hello?" she called. She stepped into the hallway, leaving the pile of decorations.

A giggle sounded behind the closed door of the far bedroom, the one with the ivy-printed wallpaper she hadn't yet explored.

"Is someone there?" she paused, her pulse fluttering. *Could it be the cops? Or new owners? What if they think I trashed this place?*

The room at the end of the hall stayed silent.

"Sorry for trespassing..." Barb trailed off, waiting for a response. When none came, she stepped toward the stairs, the floorboards groaning beneath her feet. "I'm leaving!"

"Wait!" A voice called, chiming like a bell through the humid summer air. "Don't forget your gift." The lilt of a young girl's voice faded into giggles. "Mama wants you to have it for ice cream!"

"What gift?" Barb asked, her voice no more than a whisper.

Another breeze swept through the house and nudged the two-dollar bill. It skittered across the floorboards like a dried leaf to land by the toe of her right sneaker.

"Uh, thank you," she said, softly.

"Come back tomorrow!" the girl called. "I'll show you my toys!"

Barb plucked the money from the floor and took the stairs two at a time. Once outside, she gulped a breath. *What just happened?* Out of instinct, she looked around for Tommy Legge and his gang—they were probably off stoning frogs by the dam or pretending to drown at the lake, all in good fun to get a rise out of the poor lifeguard.

The ice cream truck rounded her corner, and after a moment's thought, she flagged him down, trading the two-dollar bill for a Choco Taco. Sensing the prickle of eyes on her back, she bit into the crunchy shell and turned, watching the windows of Ghost House. No faces or dancing shadows appeared as Barb savored the sweet melt of ice cream and chocolate on her tongue.

All night she thought of the voice, of the phantom breeze pushing the dollar toward her. She tossed, throwing her covers this way and that, and came up with reasons for why she must've imagined it.

It was hot, she thought. *I probably imagined it. Hallucinations, like the mirages people see crossing the desert.* But she remembered the giggle. The echo of it ricocheted within her chest, and she didn't sleep much at all that night.

The next morning, Barb beelined for Ghost House only to be intercepted by Tommy and his pack of assholes.

"Barbarian!" Tommy shouted as she crossed the street. He rode up on his yellow BMX, popping a wheelie to mount the curb. She kept her gaze down and moved to pass him, but his friends circled closer.

"Hey Barbara! Going to Hulk out on us today?" Tommy smiled, proud to reference that craptastic day last spring when she ripped the seat of her shorts in gym class. She'd known they were too small, but her mom never stopped whining that Barb was outgrowing things quicker than she could buy them. As soon as she realized what happened, Barb ran for the lockers, but not before she caught sight of Tommy reenacting the event as if she was the Incredible Hulk busting through her clothes and preparing for a rampage.

"Leave me alone, Tommy," she muttered, crossing her arms over her boobs. She bet that'd be the next subject of ridicule.

To her surprise, Tommy pivoted his bike to the side and let her pass. She broke off in a sprint toward Ghost House.

"Don't run too fast, Barbarian!" Tommy yelled. "You'll give yourself a black eye with those knockers." His friends cackled as Barb's face heated.

In the shadows of Ghost House, Barb took a breath and closed the back door behind her, shouldering it in place against the frame. Through one of the shattered windows, she watched Tommy and his friends circle closer and then ride off down the sidewalk.

27

"Asshole," she muttered, spitting the word out the same way her mom would when getting cut off on the interstate.

The calm embrace of Ghost House enveloped her, and she straightened her spine, relishing the stretch—no need to slump or make herself look smaller here. She was alone and could do as she pleased.

Actually . . . Barb paused, heart racing as she soaked in the silence.

"Hello?" she called from the empty kitchen, her voice pitchy with nerves. She faced the stairs. "Anyone here?"

Nothing.

She headed upstairs, looking toward the shut door of the ivy-wallpapered room. She stepped into the bedroom she'd abandoned and froze. Garlands now decorated the walls and the color wheel lamp was propped up. The stockings hung limp, tacked onto the windowsill.

"You came back!" A girl's voice echoed from down the hall. A shadow shifted through the gloom and wavered in the air, the rough silhouette of a small person barely up to Barb's chest. It drew closer, and Barb felt cobwebs of static cross her skin. The color wheel lamp started spinning, releasing a clicking noise that kept pace with Barb's racing pulse.

"Do you want to see my toys?" the shadow asked.

Barb swallowed, struggling to form words.

"Come," the girl called. The shadow retreated, disappearing into the ivy room. The color wheel lamp creaked to a halt. Barb took one last look at the stairs and followed.

Sun filled the room with a golden glow, and the shadow girl took shape as if the light itself fed her color. She wore her auburn hair in ringlets against a faded cornflower blue dress. Her skin was equally pale, sickly even. This close, Barb could see the child's gaunt cheeks and the shadows under her sunken eyes. Waxy, pallid skin and thin colorless lips.

Despite her appearance, she shared a soft, kind smile and watched Barb with a bright gaze as she plopped down on the floor beside a tea set and beckoned for her to sit. "It's not polite to stare, you know." Her pale cheeks took on a rosy hue as if she was blushing, even in death.

"Sorry." Barb quickly looked away, taking a seat crisscross applesauce beside her. *I'm having tea with a ghost*, she thought as the girl smiled up at her. *A friggin' ghost.*

"Sugar?" the ghost girl asked, pouring some imaginary tea from the dusty pot into a star-speckled cup. Barb tried not to stare too hard as her host seemed to flicker at the edges. When Barb wasn't looking directly at her, she fizzled and faded in her peripherals.

The ghost girl passed Barb an empty teacup. "Your name's Barbara?"

"Barb," she said automatically.

The ghost wrinkled her nose. "Barbara *is* an old lady name. Everyone calls me Barbie."

Pieces clicked together in Barb's mind. "The stocking was yours?"

The girl reached for a flopped-over doll, pressing a cup to its lips. "Mama says I'm named after my great grandma." She squinted and leaned closer. "Old lady name, see?"

Barb nodded, still not believing this ghost girl was chatting her up like a favorite babysitter.

Barb's next words escaped without a thought: "What happened to you?"

The girl froze, her cup half raised to her lips.

"Oh, I'm sorry! I'm sorry . . ." Barb reached out to touch the girl's arm, but her hand passed through a cloud of static. Energy snapped and crackled around her fingertips as Barb flinched. "I didn't mean . . ."

"It's okay. The worst of it is over now." The ghost girl placed her cup down and hugged her doll to her chest. "I was sick, but after a little while it wasn't so bad. Just boring. I waited a long time and eventually Mama joined me." She shrugged. "We've been together ever since."

Barbie tucked the doll against Barb's thigh. "You haven't touched your tea."

29

"Oh." Barb picked up her cup and swallowed a gulp of air. "Delicious." Barbie beamed. The shadows under her eyes seemed to lighten.

Glass crashed downstairs, and they both jolted.

"What was that?"

The ghost girl rose, smoothing her dress. "I'll go look. You enjoy your tea." She nudged the doll. "Marigold is a good listener."

Within a few steps, the girl dissolved into shadow and disappeared around the doorway.

Barb waited, watching dust float by in the sun. The house stayed silent. She shifted uneasily, uncrossing and recrossing her legs. After a moment, footsteps sounded on the stairs, then in the hallway. They came to a stop outside the door to Barbie's room.

"What was it?" Barb called, waiting for the ghost girl to run in. "Barbie?"

Tommy Legge stepped forward and stood smirking in the doorframe. "Talking to yourself, Barbarian?" He surveyed the tea set. "A party! Mind if I join?"

Tommy stepped into the room and shut the door behind him. Barb pushed herself to her feet.

"Leave me alone, Tommy." Her voice trembled, and her hands clenched into clammy fists as he stepped closer. She was taller than him, sure, but he was stocky and used to a fight. Only a seventh grader, she'd seen him throw a punch at the bus stop that knocked a high school kid on his ass.

For each step he took, she retreated until her back pressed against Barbie's cluttered bookcase. Tommy kicked his way through the tea set, trampling the doll and stomping a saucer.

"I think we could be good friends," Tommy growled, reaching toward her.

She swatted him away and forced herself to stand taller. "I said quit it, Tommy." His smile never touched his eyes.

30

Behind him, the door opened slowly, silently. Shadows gathered in the hallway.

Barb's hand settled on something heavy from the shelves—a small statue of a rabbit—and she gripped it tightly. Tommy's gaze caught the movement. He released a harsh cackle.

"Barbarian, are you planning to whack me over the head and drag me back to your cave?"

He lunged forward, gripping her wrist so hard she yelped and dropped the statue. He pinned her arm against the bookcase, his breath sour and hot on her face.

The shadows shifted into the room. A smaller one flickered by the tea set and a much larger one billowed in, yawning to the ceiling and stretching to each side like raven wings.

Static filled the air as the toys littering the floor came alive. A monkey with cymbals clapped manically from the corner. A jack-in-the-box burst loose and bobbed to a tinkering melody. A teddy bear pinwheeled against the floorboards, spinning like a top toward them. Tommy turned, flinching as Marigold the doll sat up and stared at him with her black button eyes. His grip loosened on Barb's wrist. She wrenched free and used all of her force to shove him.

"I said," Barb growled, stepping toward Tommy, "leave me alone!" Tommy jolted as a toy car bounced against his foot. The shadows behind him deepened.

"What—" Before Tommy could finish the question, Barb raised her leg and planted her heel against his stomach. Doubling over, Tommy stumbled back to where the larger shadow waited. His jaw slackened as the ghost engulfed him, shadows oozing over his shoulders and enveloping his waist like a cloak of thick tar. The moppy mess of his hair stood on end. His feet rose off the floor.

Tommy floated for one still, quiet moment.

Then the shadow dragged him back through the doorway, sweeping him away on a tide of night. Tommy's screams echoed down the hall as the toys fell limp.

Beside Barb, the little ghost girl materialized and plucked Marigold from the floor. She hugged the doll to her chest.

"Mama can only hold him for so long. You better go."

Barb ran to the stairs, but a muffled scream from the previous day's bedroom made her pause. She peeked through the cracked door, glimpsing a whirl of shadow and color. Flashing Christmas lights vined around Tommy's legs and arms, garland circled his neck. The color wheel lamp spun wildly, casting a sickly, ever-shifting glow as he struggled against his bonds. His wide gaze met Barb's. Tommy screamed, his words muffled by the mouthful of tinsel.

Barb shut the door, savoring the satisfying click as the latch settled into place. Tommy's screams grew louder, harsher, as she sprinted for the stairs. She took them two at a time, grateful for her long legs, for her strength. She felt powerful, fearless, wild as she ran toward the back door's patch of sunlight. Barb dove out into the open air with a warrior's yell and landed sure-footed among the untamed weeds. Tommy's muffled cries echoed through Ghost House as she smiled and stood tall.

The Power Players of Foxtail

By A.H. Williams

Luther removed the small vial of cocaine from the secret pocket he had sewn into his custom Armani suit. He uncorked the vial and scooped a bump with the snuff spoon gifted to him by the US Ambassador to Thailand. The powder stung as he inhaled, and the restaurant bathroom around him narrowed, until it was just him, the dirty porcelain sink, and his bald reflection. Luther was ready to do business.

Luther adjusted the Windsor knot on his tie, checked his nostrils, and used a cotton handkerchief to dry and polish his scalp. The cocaine made him more sensitive to the little details. In his days as a novice user, this sensitivity could escalate to paranoia; but after a thirty-year career on Wall Street, he had attained mastery over the drug. It was a tool of the trade, no different than a carpenter's hammer or a doctor's stethoscope. And it was a tool he would need for tonight.

Luther checked each nostril one last time, then confidently burst out the door into the dining room of the Wooden Rooster. The tavern had an exuberant energy, in rhythm with Luther's high. Waitresses carried trays of espresso martinis. Busboys hustled to prepare empty tables for the next guest. Young men sat with beautiful women, telling stories of the Street. Talk of alphas, and deltas, and present values, and "while my base salary is pretty low, once my commission and bonus come in, I expect to clear six figures." Their dates nodded and laughed where they were supposed to, and tried to look appropriately impressed when they were supposed to, and did their best to look confused—but not too confused—when they were supposed to. Luther felt nostalgic, watching these young bucks peacock around.

33

Luther took his seat at the table and looked at the three other Board members finishing their final bites of dinner. He saw the still-empty fifth seat and did his best not to smile. Instead, he checked his white gold Rolex Submariner. 7:19 PM. Eleven minutes.

"Oh Luther, you're back," said Dave, gesturing with his fork. "I was just telling Kathy here about pickleball."

"Pickleball, huh," Luther said, "is that what those racquets I always see you loading into your car are for? I thought I remembered you saying they were for squash."

"Oh no, squash was last month," said Dave with a laugh, "but then I discovered pickleball. Way more fun."

"I can hardly keep up with all your hobbies," said Kathy, the Board's secretary. "Last month it was squash. Then rock climbing. Then kayaking."

Dave laughed and patted his large belly. "The Doctor says I need to lose weight, and I have the ADHD," said Dave. "It's not that I lose interest in those hobbies. I just get fired up about the next one."

"Well, it's clearly working," said Luther, "and if it's too personal, please feel free to say so but, how much weight have you lost?"

Dave smiled wide and patted his stomach. "No, no," he said, "thirty pounds, if you can believe it. Down to 310."

"That's just phenomenal."

When most people saw Dave, they saw David Willis, the Board's treasurer. A slightly overweight insurance broker who wore baggy suits in a vain attempt to conceal how overweight he was. They saw the heir to a multimillion-dollar aerospace empire, a father of three, and husband to a—well out of his league—supermodel wife. But not Luther. He saw the same things he saw when he looked at anyone. The instruments of control. The levers that pushed and pulled a person's actions. The engine that fueled their motivations. The buttons that got them out of bed in the morning, and the ones that put them to sleep at night. He had made a career out of this vision.

34

So when he looked at Dave, he saw a man desperate for validation. For any sign that he was a man truly worthy of his fortune and of his beautiful wife. That the people golfing with him were there because they want to spend time with him, not to propose some new investment opportunity. That his wife married him for the way he made her laugh, and not because of what his father gave him. A man desperate to feel worthy of a life he didn't earn. Luther provided that validation with a friendship that seemed genuine—and Dave voted accordingly.

"You have to come down to the community center and play with me some time," said Dave.

"I'll do you one better," said Luther. "At my club, the director of our pickleball program is actually competing in the World Pickleball Championship up in Boston this summer, if you could believe there is such a thing. I could bring you as my guest one day. You can test your skills against a real pro."

"That would be great!" said Dave.

"Any time. And that invitation is extended to the two of you as well," Luther said, pointing his fork at Kathy and Alejandra, the Board's Member-at-Large.

"I might have to take you up on that," said Kathy with her loud but genuine laugh. "But do I need to give it up in a month and start mountain biking to get the same results?"

"You strike me as more the yoga type," said Luther with a wink, "or Pilates, or competitive flower-picking."

Kathy laughed. "You know me too well."

When most people saw Kathy Salatino, they saw a 40-something-year-old Human Resources Director, deep in the throngs of eastern mysticism. A woman clad in crystals that she claimed warded of diseases and brought good luck. The Board saw a woman who never made a decision without consulting her horoscope or psychic. But Luther saw a woman desperate for meaning. A woman who wanted there to be a higher purpose to her years spent shuffling papers from one pile to the next. That her years settling disputes about the employee lounge and whose responsibility it was to clean out the old milk somehow had importance beyond the petty egos of middle management. That the many men she'd had throughout the years would receive some kind of cosmic justice for scorning her. Ultimately, Luther saw a woman desperate for the perfect justice, love, and mercy of God in a Godless world. Things which, of course, Luther could never provide. But he could provide her with whatever horoscope he wanted by bribing the psychic of her favorite astrology website.

Luther checked his watch. 7:23PM. Seven Minutes.

"How about you, Alejandra?" he asked as he mimed swinging a racquet. "You. Want. Play. Pickleball?"

"Oh, thank you," said Alejandra through her thick Spanish accent, "but no. I no play. My knees. You understand."

"I understand perfectly," said Luther, "but if you ever change your mind the invitation is open. If you're anywhere near the athlete your niece is, I think Dave here would be in trouble." That got another laugh from the table. Alejandra smiled wide, but Luther wasn't sure how much of what he said the old woman understood. Even with the language barrier, Luther could still see through the wrinkled Hispanic grandmother's acts of kindness to the glowing gem at the core of her actions. A gem that was a relic of a previous generation, and all but unknown in the circles that Luther walked. Love. A selfless kind of love. Love of community. Love of neighbor. And most of all, love of family. Which meant her vote required the greatest of Luther's sacrifices: her fat, ugly niece, Stephanie, who Luther had spent the past month dating.

"Also. Thank. You. For. Watering. My. Plants," said Luther, tipping over an invisible watering can.

Alejandra gave a polite half smile. Luther shrugged and lifted his Macallan 18 Year to his mouth, making sure to inhale its peaty notes before sipping. Not bad. He preferred the 24 Year, but—excluding

36

Dave—he knew none of the other board members could afford a restaurant that served it. Now that he was the Board's president, he planned on taking them out to Dominick's once or twice a year as a treat.

Luther looked down at his timepiece. 7:25 PM. "Okay, five minutes," he said. "Guess we'll have to start without Julia." He waved down their cute brunette server who was in the middle of taking a different table's order. Luther snapped his fingers and shouted. "Excuse me? Can you please clear out the plates? We have a very important meeting that starts in five minutes."

The cute brunette server smiled an imitation of a smile at Luther. A short, stout busboy happened to be passing by, and she pointed him toward Luther's table. The boy took the plates away, and the Board replaced them with their laptops.

As the host, Luther hovered his cursor over the 'Start Meeting' button. "Are you all ready to get started?"

The other three nodded. Luther clicked his mouse, and his screen changed to four boxes with each Board member's face, giving a panoramic view of their table. In the bottom corner, a counter indicated twenty spectators.

"Hello everyone," said Luther, "Welcome to the October 12th, 2023 meeting of the Foxtail Condo HOA Board. If you do not already know, Mrs. Walter has stepped down after three years of service to our community, to spend more time with her grandchildren. As your duly elected vice president, I will assume her duties, and am now your acting president," Luther paused for applause that never came, cleared his throat and continued. "It is on the agenda tonight to decide when we will hold elections for a new vice president. But before all that, let me introduce the rest of the Board. I am joined by your treasurer, David Willis."

"Hi everybody," said Dave, his hand a pixelated blur as he smiled and waved.

"By your secretary, Kathy Salatino."

Kathy brought a peace sign up to her cheek.

"And by our member-at-large, Alejandra Mariscal."

Alejandra gave a short smile.

"Our community events organizer, Julia Campbell, got caught up and is unable to attend tonight's meeting," said Luther, once again repressing a smile. "Okay Dave, why don't you kick things off—"

"Sorry I'm late," said a deep female voice. Luther's mouth bent into a scowl as he watched Julia set her laptop down at the table's empty seat; but he caught himself and forced his lips into a smile that looked like the one the cute brunette waitress had given him earlier.

"Oh, never mind," Luther said to his virtual audience, "Julia managed to make it after all."

"Please, go ahead, get started without me," Julia said, taking a pull from her pink electronic cigarette.

"Not a problem," said Luther, "David was just about to start us off." Luther nodded toward Dave, who began by reminding everyone of the HOA's Quiet Hours Policy, then provided a brief update on the cracked sidewalk near the front gate. When he started talking about the group of teenagers loitering outside units 1251 and 1261, a fifth box appeared in the chat containing the purple hair and pierced face of Julia Campbell. But that's not what Luther saw. Though they couldn't be from more different worlds, Luther saw the same thing he saw when he looked in the mirror of the Wooden Rooster's bathroom: a person with an insatiable hunger for power. For control. Whether it was within the high rises of Wall Street, or the city's most popular open-mic slam poetry nights. And now those forces battled for control of the Foxtail Condominium Complex Homeowners Association. In Julia, Luther saw the face of a person who would do everything and anything to dominate the people around her.

"I'd like to propose a motion," said Julia.

Luther looked over to Julia, a skeptical look in his eyes.

"Um . . . sure," he said, "you are recognized."

"I propose a vote amongst the committee for the role of interim president."

Luther coughed up his scotch. "What? No, no, no. I'm the interim president. That's the whole point of a vice president. When the president is absent, the vp acts in his place."

Julia smiled, pulled out a sheet of paper from her bag, and cleared her throat. "According to Section IV of the Committee Bylaws, 'In the event that the president steps down, the vice president will assume the duties of president—"

"Exactly!" Luther said, thudding his scotch onto the table.

"Alternatively," Julia continued, "the Board may vote on the president. Members may nominate themselves, but must receive a three-fifths majority to assume the role."

Luther stared at his scotch, his thoughts racing. "Okay well, your motion needs to be second—"

"Seconded," said Dave, his eyes fixated on the table.

Luther turned and stared daggers at David, who continued to stare at the table. Luther craned his neck toward Julia and stared into the face of a cat with its mouse cornered. He should've known the sneaky bitch would try some last-minute power play, just like she did with the hedges in 2018. Luther still felt hatred rise up whenever he passed those petunias.

"Okay, then," Luther said, "I nominate myself as president. Any other takers?"

Julia's hand shot up. "I also nominate myself."

The chatroom chimed as the spectator count increased to twenty-two, word of the coup no doubt spreading through the neighborhood. Luther took a deep breath and gathered himself. He scanned Dave, Kathy, and Alejandra; knowing a shark like Julia wouldn't make a move like this without the absolute assurance that she had the votes. Dave still couldn't make eye contact with him, while Kathy made herself familiar with the ceiling. Alejandra looked from person to person, seemingly unsure of what was happening. Luther nodded to himself. Now he knew where all the pieces were. The only question was his next move. "Okay, anybody else?" Luther asked. "Dave? You interested in the role?"

"No," said Dave, nearly choking on the word.

"How about you, Kathy?"

"You're stalling," said Julia. "Let's start the vote."

"Now hold on," said Luther, "let's make sure everyone gets a chance to voice their interest. Kathy, you interested?"

"Who, me?" said Kathy. "You kidding? I can't be trusted with that much responsibility."

"Perfect, so me and Luther," said Julia. "Why don't we start the votes so everyone can get on with their night?"

Luther felt his anger swell as the laptops continued to chime, the counter increasing to twenty-five. Then it dawned on him.

"Yeah, sure," said Luther, as he creeped his hand to his mousepad, "let's start the vote."

He moved his cursor over the 'End Meeting' button and clicked. The program asked, *Are you sure? This will end the meeting for all parties.* He hovered over the 'Yes' button and looked to the rest of the table. "Okay, all members for myself, please say—" Luther pushed the button. There was a beep, and the chat room vanished.

"Oh no," Luther said, "it seems we've lost connection."

"Oh please, Luther," Julia said, "this is ridiculous."

"What?" said Luther, grasping at invisible pearls. "It's the Wi-Fi in this place. Always spotty."

"My connection's fine," said Dave.

"Well maybe it's my old laptop then," Luther said. "Just let me reboot it and I'll send out the invites again."

"Don't bother," said Julia, "I'll do it. Just send me the email list of everyone in the complex."

"Too late. I already restarted my computer," said Luther, giving his best impression of a man restarting his laptop.

Julia crossed her flabby arms and took a long pull from her e-cigarette, her shoulders relaxing as she exhaled. "Fine," she said, "but hurry up."

"Of course," said Luther, turning to Dave who still looked like a puppy caught peeing on the carpet by its owner. "You know, Dave, I was thinking about all that pickleball talk from earlier. And that World Pickleball Championship up in Boston this summer. We should buy tickets and head up there together."

Dave's eyes widened. He turned toward Luther, though he kept his head down toward the table. "Re—really?" he said.

"Sure," said Luther, "what could be better than spending the weekend with one of my closest friends, watching a phenomenal sport?"

"Yeah," said Dave, excitement creeping into his voice, "that would be awesome."

"Oh, were we talking pickleball earlier?" asked Julia. "I used to play in college. If you guys are going to the championship, I would totally be down."

"To be honest, Julia," said Luther, "I think Dave's wife and my Stephanie would be uncomfortable with us going up to Boston with a beautiful young lady like yourself. I think it's going to have to be a guy's trip."

Dave nodded in agreement. "Yeah, sorry Julia," he said. "Veronica doesn't like me going away on trips with other women unless she can come."

"Makes perfect sense," said Luther with a smile, "a handsome man like yourself. She's right to worry." Then he clinked his glass with Dave. "To the pickleballers of Foxtail."

Luther sipped his scotch and savored notes of pepper and victory. "Oh, would you look at that," he said, "my computer's back up."

41

Luther re-sent the invitations, this time thirty-one people accepting it; a record attendance.

"I'm so sorry about that everyone," Luther said, "The Wi-Fi at this tavern is shoddy. I'll do my best to speed this meeting along. When we got disconnected, the Board was about to vote for the interim president. The nominees were myself, of course, and Julia. We'll get right to it. All in favor of Julia becoming the interim president?"

Julia's hand was up first, "Aye."

Kathy's hand was next in the air. "Aye," she said.

Luther wondered what Kathy had been promised in return for her vote. Most likely Julia had agreed to switch to that organic pesticide that Kathy had been sharing articles about on the local town Facebook group. Then Luther looked to Dave, who gave an exaggerated wink, which Luther happily returned. He wasn't sure what Dave had been promised, but whatever it was, there was no chance it was more valuable than a boy's weekend in Boston. Luther smiled and took a long pull of scotch.

"Aye."

Luther slammed his glass of scotch on the table. His head spun toward the voice to see the wrinkled hand of Alejandra raised in the air.

"Wh—Why?" he quivered.

Alejandra shook her head, thin skin gliding over muscle and bone. But her eyes animated with a hatred that seemed younger than her true age.

"Why?" he asked again, "why?" Each time the question getting less confused and angrier. "Why? How could you do this to me, Alejandra! I'm dating your niece, for Christ's sake. How could you turn on me like this?"

"Last Sunday," she said.

"What?" said Luther.

"Last Sunday," she said, this time with more emphasis. "Last Sunday, I think you still out of town. I come to water you fancy tree plant," she jabbed a finger at Kathy. "I walk in on you fucking this puta."

"What?" Kathy said.

"Alejandra, please," said Luther, "this has got to be some kind of misunderstanding." But Kathy flushed a shade of red as damning as any confession. The computers chimed as several more residents joined the chat.

Julia shaded her face with her hand, partly to hide from the awkwardness at the table, partly to hide the pure joy on her face. This was better than anything she could have hoped for.

"No, no, no," Luther said. He pushed his seat back and slammed his scotch down on the table, shattering the glass and hushing the conversations at all the adjacent tables. "You pit of vipers," Luther spat. "After all I've done for this community. After all I've done for you personally."

He jabbed a finger at Alejandra. "You! Who covered for you when you wanted to move our meetings to Thursday nights instead of Mondays, because you wanted to 'see your grandkids play soccer.' I know you're just getting wine drunk and watching your soap operas."

Alejandra shouted at Luther in Spanish that was way too quick to follow, so he turned to Julia.

"And Julia," he said, "why don't you tell Alejandra why the cops can't catch the kids smoking pot and leaving beer cans outside her unit? Because there aren't any kids. It's just you and your degenerate, loser friends."

"That's a lie!" Julia said, nervously eyeing Alejandra, who paused her tirade, but only briefly, before she resumed launching a steady stream of insults at both Luther and Julia. Kathy, meanwhile, took deep breaths, muttering a quiet mantra, trying to find her inner peace amongst all this chaos.

"Hey Luther," said Dave, patting him on the shoulder, "maybe we should calm do—"

"Oh, shut the fuck up, Dave," Luther said, loud enough to silence the tables next to them. "How about that time I caught you and your 'friend from work' skinny dipping in the hot tub? I didn't say a thing to anyone. Not your wife. Not the Board. And you just tried to cross me? You're pathetic. So just shut the fuck up."

Alejandra and Kathy looked at Dave. Dave flushed red, but kept his eyes on the table, where their laptops sounded like wind chimes in a rainstorm as more and more residents joined the chatroom. Julia slipped off one of her red Converse sneakers to smack on the table like a judge's gavel. "Luther, that's enough. You're acting like a child."

"I am not!" Luther smacked the table back. "I am acting like a man being denied what is rightfully his, you fat . . ." He stopped halfway, noticing his laptop screen. 104 in attendance. By far, the largest meeting they'd ever had. Luther wiped the rage sweat from his forehead, slammed his laptop shut, and stormed out of the restaurant, leaving the rest of the Board with their secrets laid bare.

Dave cleared his throat and timidly opened his mouth to speak.

"Are we still on for pickleball?"

The Eyesore
By Sharbari Ahmed

The Duttas moved in on a snowy Sunday. The wind chill froze the pipes of their new home. When Krishna Dutta flushed the toilet in the basement—his first piss in the house—the pipes, installed in 1934, burst and flooded his basement with an eighth of an inch of brown water. He didn't want to speculate why the water was brown. This fetid water then mysteriously bubbled up, seeping into the front lawn, rising through the snow, defying, in Krishna's mind, physics.

Perhaps, he thought, shit floats in Connecticut. To his dismay, the pristine powder surrounding the small, white-painted brick house now looked like a mushy septic trench.

He didn't relish spending six hundred dollars, but it was a Sunday. Pipes were bursting all over town. He was in no position to bargain. Krishna was a self-effacing man, thirty-seven years of age, lanky, tall, and prematurely greying. His wife, Farzana, and he met in college in New Delhi, their third year. They were forced to elope because he was a Hindu, and she was a Muslim from Bangladesh. His parents were Brahmins, both lawyers; hers was a middle-class family from Dhaka. Her mother, a pediatrician with a modest practice, earned more money than Farzana's father, a manager at a jute refining factory. They were immensely proud of their daughter, whose academic achievements exceeded their wildest expectations. Until she married the Hindu boy. Then they wondered what they had done to deserve such a calamity.

The couple had chosen to move to Connecticut because they wanted children, and where they lived in New York City did not have the school system they were hoping for. Both Krish and Farzana worked as middle managers at Deloitte and General Electric,

45

respectively. When Krish was laid off, they could no longer afford more than a one-bedroom apartment in Queens. This would not do, as they both hoped that their respective sets of parents would someday come to visit and stay for months at a time. Ten years on, neither sets of parents were willing to forgive their children for stepping out of the fold. They bought the house anyway, right after the Covid pandemic eased, with the hope that being forcibly separated would have softened their families' hearts.

They chose the town of Darien and overpaid by about 50K. It was the smallest house on the block, three bedrooms and only one full working bathroom, with a powder room off the pokey wood-paneled den that had not been touched since 1978. The realtor had not even counted the bathroom in the basement since it didn't appear to be a working toilet.

Krish secured a job in Stamford. There were many Bangladeshi families in Stamford. Farzana noted that the majority of Bangladeshis lived off exit 6 on the 1-95, in apartments and multifamily houses with rusty chain link fences delineating the properties. Farzana noted that Indians, with Teslas, and BMWs were aplenty in Darien. As far as she could tell, there were few chain link fences.

Farzana was more pragmatic than her husband, and when he balked at the price for the pipe repair, and wanted to look for a different quote, she pointed out that the gray pool forming in their front yard was not an auspicious introduction to the neighborhood.

As they were arguing in their mild way, the doorbell rang. It was faint; they did not hear it at first. They both stared up at the sky, wondering where the chiming was coming from.

"Is that the front door or the back door?" she asked him. "Wasn't that supposed to be fixed?" she said, moving toward the front door. There was no accusation in her voice, but Krishna felt guilty. He already regretted buying the house. It was an uncharacteristically impulsive move on his part. Marrying Farzana was the most daring thing he had ever done, and he didn't allow himself to regret that, even when his father stormed out of the house after he told them he had married a Muslim girl. His father was not sure what was worse—that Krishna had married a Muslim, or that he had married a Bangladeshi.

On their cracked concrete stoop stood Archita Acharya, PMP (Project Management Professional), a forty-seven-year-old, round-eyed, and bespectacled architect from New Delhi, who had moved to Connecticut fourteen years prior, and had appointed herself a sort of mayor of the immediate neighborhood. A proud Brahmin, who pretended caste did not matter to her, she was the president and founder of the South Asian Association of Southern Connecticut, always running unchallenged. She also served on the PTA and sat on the board of the Friends of Noroton Woods and Tilley Pond, two parks in the north part of town. She was a naturalized citizen of seven years, and a registered Republican, with local political aspirations. She weighed in on various topics on Facebook—even if she was not well-versed on them, because she did not relish being left out of the loop.

Archita was a polarizing presence in town—garnering both praise and searing indictment. Her outward self-confidence masked a niggling notion that the wealthy, white residents of the town secretly laughed at her behind her back. She was not misguided. There were quite a few white folks who found her audacity off-putting. She inserted herself into nearly every conversation involving town politics and operations, be it parking issues at the high school, or the ammonia created from too much goose shit in Tilley Pond Park. They would not admit this readily, but it seemed she somehow forgot her place on the ethnic pecking order.

They didn't know that Archita's commanding father, who withheld affection and was also an architect of some success back in India, compelled her to focus on attaining status wherever she went.

Archita held a box of Indian *mithai*—sweets to welcome the couple into town—that she had purchased in Edison, New Jersey and frozen in her subzero Viking for six months for such an occasion. Archita's eyes were her most striking feature. Her pupils appeared constantly dilated and the eyeballs jutted out a little, giving her a look of perpetual surprise or judgment. Given Archita's nature, it was often the latter. A well-meaning neighbor once asked if she had a thyroid condition because of her slightly bulging eyes. She didn't. She was plump, having never lost what she gained from two pregnancies. Archita's round eyes glided swiftly over Farzana's slim frame, making the younger woman self-conscious almost immediately.

Farzana tugged at the neck of her blue sweater. She was embarrassed by the state of the lawn. A flash of irrational resentment towards Krish for flushing the toilet in the basement radiated into her thoughts.

She opened her mouth to speak but Archita spoke first. She assessed quickly that Farzana was not self-assured. Given the state of the front lawn, it wasn't a surprise.

"Welcome to the neighborhood," Archita said, holding out the box of sweets. Farzana took the proffered box and gave Archita a wan smile as thanks. She opened her mouth to speak, but Archita once again spoke over her. "Svagate he," she said in Hindi. "I'm Archita. Acharya."

Farzana smiled, embarrassed. "I'm sorry," she said. "I speak Bangla. I know very little Hindi. I mean, I understand some—I'm Farzana."

Archita raised her eyebrows. "You're not Indian?" To Farzana it sounded like an accusation. Before she could reply Archita said, "Oh, you're from Cal?"

"No, Dhaka originally," Farzana replied. "Actually, my parents are from Chittagong, but settled in Dhaka."

"Oh, Bangladeshi? So, Muslim?"

Archita's throat tightened. When she was 15, she had fallen in love with a Muslim boy, and her family had objected so strongly, they shipped her off to boarding school in Darjeeling, in hopes she would

48

forget him. By the time she had come back home, he had moved on and seemed surprised that she had held on to her feelings for him.

Farzana, baffled by the sudden tightening of the air, said, 'I'm a non- practicing Muslim, but please don't tell my mother." Her joke fell with a thud, as Archita looked past her, into the tiny foyer. The flowery, metallic wallpaper was torn and peeling. Farzana tried to block her view by moving in front of her.

Archita, who was taller, moved up a step, peering further down the hall. She had been in the house many times but wanted to see if any improvements had been made. So far, none that she could discern.

"I had heard you were both from New Delhi. Like me."

Farzana wondered where she would have heard this. Archita made it a point to know most of the realtors in town.

"I said welcome," Archita said, when Farzana did not invite her in. "That was Hindi for welcome. Svagate he."

She pushed her thick glasses up the bridge of her flat nose. It was an exercise in futility, as the glasses promptly slid down the bridge and rested almost at the end. Farzana noticed the oily sheen on the bridge of Archita's flat nose. She wondered how she kept the glasses balanced on it. Archita mostly let them sit at the end. They constricted her nostrils, making it sound like she was always congested.

Archita fanned herself with her hand, even though it was forty degrees outside. She was annoyed that this slip of a girl was not inviting her in. A thought struck her.

"Don't worry," she said. "My place is a mess. I am renovating," she added, in her best breezy tone.

Archita had started renovations on her 18th-century farmhouse years earlier. When her investment banker husband was laid off, she ran out of money and started looking for ways to fund her projects.

She lobbied to have the Duttas' small, white-painted brick house torn down. It ruined the clipped uniformity of the neighborhood. It was the only house that was not a colonial. Archita was not sure what the style was. It was built in the '30s. It was not mid-century. It was not a ranch. It was not a bungalow. It was a squat, square abomination, a character-less pile of hastily painted bricks that sullied the otherwise attractive surroundings.

She had proposed to design a house that fit into the esthetic of the neighborhood and would find a developer who would be willing to pay her to oversee the design and building of it. Modern colonial farmhouse was all the rage. The plan was set in motion, but the original owners became sentimental and stalled the demolition, citing that it had been in the family for decades and could be salvaged. While the situation was held up in zoning hell, the family, the Gundersons, had sold it to the Duttas, without so much as a by-your-leave to Archita, who took the matter personally, because Archita took most things personally.

"Dutta is not a Mus—it's a Bengali name," Archita said, catching herself. She was wary of being precipitous. Her teacher in grade 9 told her she was too precipitous, and Archita, naturally, took it personally. She giggled. "I have many Bengali friends." (She had one, who no longer spoke to her). "I love Bengalis." (She found them all snooty. They thought they were superior to all other South Asians.) "I have always wanted to visit Bangladesh." (This was a bald-faced lie. Like most Indians of her milieu, Bangladesh was either not on their radar or it was dismissed as an abysmal, backward country, with nothing to recommend it except muslin saris and fish curry.)

Krishna appeared behind Farzana, who had not been able to interject much. Archita's eyes lit up in surprise. Krishna was awkward but striking.

"Please come in," Krishna said, before Farzana could stop him. "I'm Krishna." She nearly cried out. She had no reasonable explanation for it, but she knew that letting Archita in was somehow dangerous. She quickly stymied the thought. When they had called the emergency plumbers, she had a brief moment where she was not sure she wanted even service people to see the decrepitude of their surroundings. There was something about Darien that made it seem like a mess of any kind would not be tolerated.

Once invited, Archita walked into the narrow entrance hallway without hesitation, and it was all she could do to keep from grimacing at the garish '80s metallic wallpaper and scuffed, dull wooden floor. She was clearly familiar with the house. This further unsettled Farzana.

"The floor can be salvaged, you know?" she said to Farzana and tapped her toe lightly on the boards. "Nothing beats original wood." She almost let it slip that she had previous plans for the wood floor. She was going to use it to line the cathedral ceiling in the great room of the house this couple had so unceremoniously prevented her from building.

"Oh, I see," Farzana said. Her heart began to race. The house suddenly seemed far worse than she originally thought, now that she had let Archita in. But there was no going back. She reluctantly followed Archita into the yellow linoleum-floored kitchen and offered her tea.

"Arre, no!" Archita said. "You are all so busy. I just wanted to drop by quickly and see if you needed anything." She glanced at the outdated cabinets, and then turned to Farzana, smiling brightly.

"So, I am sure you are going to gut the place?"

Though her tone suggested it was a question, neither Farzana nor Krishna were sure that it wasn't rhetorical. They looked at one another. Krish decided to answer.

"Not yet. We wanted to settle in and make changes and repairs slowly. We moved in—" he glanced at his phone, "about five hours ago."

Archita's glasses slid down her oily nose to rest at the tip. She looked over the rims at Krishna.

"You're going to live with these cabinets? You'll go mad."

Krishna coughed, glancing at Farzana, who appeared stunned at the level of rudeness directed at them.

"You'll find that after living in Darien—even for a short time—you will become allergic to ugly things," Archita added by way of explanation. She pointed out the window.

"See that colonial on the corner?" The couple nodded.

"Well, it was torn down and built back from the ground up. I designed it," she said, proudly. "It was my idea to place fireplaces on either end of the house, for symmetry. You should have seen it before. It was an eyesore."

The word hung in the air, "eyesore." Krishna decided not to reach for it, but Farzana did. She grabbed the word and tucked it away for later when she would wonder if Archita felt the same about their presence in the neighborhood.

"It looks expensive," Krishna said after a moment. "1.5," Archita sniffed.

"Mi—million?" Farzana said.

This was another Archita exaggeration, though not too far off. It was sold, after much bidding, for 1.34 million dollars and had no land to speak of. Less than half an acre. Her commission had been tidy, but she had blown it all on the addition she insisted on building to the back of her draughty colonial where she told people George Washington had stayed overnight. It was actually Aaron Burr who'd laid his head down for one night in 1776, but that was too controversial, given the recent popularity of *Hamilton*. Archita kept abreast of such things.

"So many Desis are moving into town these days. Pretty soon, we'll be the majority minority," Archita said.

This woman made Farzana uneasy in a way she had not felt since she had first told her parents about Krishna. Her fear at disappointing them when they had worked so hard to pay for her school fees had nearly driven her to a nervous breakdown. Krishna's gentle insistence that their love would find a way won out in the end. Now she was wondering why she had let him talk her into moving to this town obsessed with real estate. They had never been a flashy couple.

Farzana was suddenly not sure she could keep up with the Joneses, or in this case the Patils, Pandits, Goswamis, and Desais, or whatever other Tesla-driving Brahmins were in the mix.

Archita, for her part, was starting to look at the couple as another project she could sink her teeth into; people she could fashion into allies. She would mentor them into having social capital. They would be added to the growing phalanx of supporters in town, who would eventually vote her in as alderman. They were an unexpected couple, a Hindu, and a Muslim—from Bangladesh—but Archita would find a way to spin that into something fascinating.

If the couple had a glimpse into the workings of Archita's mind as they stood in their outdated kitchen, they would have been alarmed. Archita had not had an orgasm in six years, feeding her manic need for control. Lust and regret were so tightly packed inside her plump frame with no outlet, that she could no longer engage calmly in the world. Everything was urgent and intense, teetering on a disaster requiring her expert interference to avert cataclysm. They could not know that she was sizing them up with that same intensity and urgency. They had just wanted to move to a town with good schools, a bit of a garden, and enough space to host two sets of parents (at different times). At least that was their dream—to be forgiven for disappointing their mutually prejudicial families by buying a house. It would be a sign of their permanence.

"Acha, teek hay," Archita said, and slapped her hands on the front of her pants. "That's Hindi for ok," she said to Farzana, who knew what that meant. Farzana nodded, relieved that it seemed like the woman was going to leave.

"I'll take that cup of tea."

Farzana blinked several times. Inside, her guts churned. She looked at Krish, pleading silently. Archita sat down at their secondhand breakfast table and looked up at them. "No sugar, please. Do you have almond milk?"

"No, we don't. Have that," Farzana said. "Sorry."

"No worries, licker is fine," Archita said. She sat back, suddenly struck by nostalgia. "I have not used that word in years! If I said that to Americans, they would be confused. They would think I wanted gin with my earl grey." She stopped and looked up at Farzana. "You know what it means, right?"

Farzana nodded. "Black tea, yes." She put the electric kettle on, her back to Archita, and closed her eyes. She hoped for a miracle and then it came, in the form of Scott Rizzoli, the plumber. The faint doorbell rang. Before Krish could react, she all but ran to it and opened the door. Scott appeared nonplussed by what he saw in the front yard.

"Man, I wish you called earlier," he said. "I know we gave you an estimate, but this might be a bigger job than we thought. I'm not saying for sure it will cost more, but it might."

"Come in, please! The problem is in the basement toilet," Farzana said.

Scott walked in after wiping his feet on the doormat, something Archita had not bothered to do. "There's a basement toilet? Man, I remember this place. It was going to be torn down—oh hey Archie!"

Archita had just been served her tea by Krishna. She shook Scott's hand. "Scott! Good to see you," she said. "You were right about the septic system I ordered. Top notch."

"Archie," Scott said, "I thought you were first in line to get this house torn down. But I guess it found its family." He then beamed, inexplicably, at everyone in the now-overcrowded kitchen. When no one said anything, he shrugged. "Okay, let's get a look at that basement."

Krish, who puffed out his chest to appear less skinny, led Scott down the narrow stairs into the basement, leaving Farzana alone with Archita.

"This town is a close-knit community," Archita said. She took another sip of tea. "Word of advice, get on a first-name basis with all the blue-collar service people. They're very simple and just want to be acknowledged. It will keep you from getting fleeced. You'll still be charged Darien prices. This isn't Bridgeport."

Farzana watched as Archita took her last sip of tea and made her way to the door, still chatting. Relief settled in.

"I'll drop an invite for the South Asian Association of Southern Connecticut's end-of-year gala. We don't do it in December, when everyone is throwing galas."

Farzana wondered why so many galas were being thrown, but didn't ask, fearing more conversation.

"Tickets are steep, but I'm inviting you this time. I'm the president, after all, I should be able to sneak in a young couple," Archita continued.

Farzana nodded.

"It's all vegetarian food," Archita said, suddenly earnest. "You understand, no? For the sensitive types."

"There are no Muslims in the group?" Farzana asked.

Archita's round eyes narrowed. "Of course, there are. But since they are in the minority, we just make it all veg—to be safe."

Something in Archita's tone irked Farzana. "So, it is primarily a Hindu group?" She asked.

"Not at all," Archita said, immediately offended. "My best friend, Shahnaz Khan, is the vice president of the group." In fact, Archita and her cohorts had been steadily trying to root out Shahnaz for years, who was most-assuredly not her best friend, but this small fact she kept from Farzana.

"Shahnaz is a writer. Divorced and very smart. But opinionated. Oh, she's from Dhaka, but raised here! I forgot. Anyway, I think Krish would appreciate meeting others in *his* community," Archita added.

After she left, Farzana leaned against the door and closed her eyes.

"Scott says it's not a big problem. He'll install a sump pump to keep it from flooding again. It should cost about—" Krishna stopped and stared at Farzana who was still leaning against the door. "What's the matter?"

Farzana opened her eyes. "Can you promise me we will not join the South Asian Association of Southern Connecticut?"

"You know I don't like these organized groups. It's all gossipy and what not." Krishna walked into the kitchen.

"I'm so glad she's left," Farzana said.

Krish was surprised. "Really? I thought she was nice. So friendly." He popped one of the thawed sweet meats she had brought into his mouth. When Farzana turned her back, he spat it back into his hand. Freezer burn.

Scott emerged from the basement and quoted a price well above what they had been initially told. To Farzana's shock, Krishna did not argue.

"Archie is great," Scott said. "She's a good resource."

Farzana wondered what he would think had he known she referred to him as a simple blue-collar worker. Farzana watched Krish make out the check, thinking that men rarely understood anything going on around them, and wondered if she could convince her husband to sell the house and move away. But as she watched her sweet husband happily chat about sump pumps and sewage, chest still puffed out, she knew that his objective to put down roots just in case their parents forgave them was always a priority.

After Scott left, Krish brought Farzana tea. He put his arm around her and looked over their unattractive den. "You know, Archita was right. We would have to put on an addition when Ammi and Baba, and of course your parents, want to come and stay months at a time."

Archita had said nothing of the kind. Farzana knew that she would rather they raze their little eyesore to the ground. Farzana sipped her tea. She couldn't shake the fleeting thought—or perhaps it was a premonition—that somehow her marriage may not survive an addition of any sort.

Unfortunately

By David Sheskin

This morning I received another rejection slip. This makes twenty-eight times that *The Menopausal Analyst* has been turned down. And what of *The Libra Who Loved Szechwan Food*? Well, it has been rejected on twenty-three occasions—or is it twenty-four? And then there is my favorite story, *Hybrid Hens*, a charming but ironical exposition on the eccentricities of puberty. For some inexplicable reason this little gem has been returned to me seventeen times. But why go on? The fact of the matter is, the rejections are finally getting to me.

I am a writer. At least I like to think I am. But to be perfectly honest, it gets harder and harder to nurture that particular belief when every week approximately eight more rejection slips arrive in the mail. Most of the time the slips consist of impersonal replies printed on small slips of paper. On rare occasions some editor notes in script something to the effect that my story contained some interesting ideas or that he found it humorous, and that he'd be interested in seeing some more of my work. But, more often than not, the editors say nothing. Some, in fact, don't even bother to include a rejection slip, and this is something I find particularly annoying.

Since embarking on this ludicrous adventure, I've always harbored the belief that it is equitable to expect reimbursement for one's efforts. In view of this, until recently it has been my policy to submit my work only to those publications which offer one remuneration. But I must admit that over the past few months my resolve has weakened. After 1,141 rejection slips even the best of men are forced to compromise their standards. And, of course, there was also my wife—a pragmatic woman who earns her living counseling deranged human beings. Night after night she told me that my first priority should be to get published, and not any monetary gains that might accrue from my efforts. So, finally, I swallowed my pride and sent one particular manuscript, which by then was faded and dog-eared, to an obscure little biannual which only pays in contributor's copies.

The address of this little publication is some communal farm located outside of Walla Walla, Washington, which happens to be run by an ex-alcoholic who spends the better part of his waking hours milking cows, growing pot, and reading the literary creations of would-be writers who have exhausted all other avenues of expression. Six months later, this so-called editor sends me a letter (which I swear is soiled with the milk of some four-legged animal) that says I certainly have an interesting head, and that he'd really like to publish my story, but unfortunately *The Hypotenuse of Queen Victoria's Nose* is a bit too wordy and far too esoteric for a modest little publication such as his. And he suggests that I really shouldn't be too upset by his letter because anybody who writes the way I do certainly has talent and is bound to get published sooner or later. And, by the way, he tells me, if I ever happen to be passing through the Pacific Northwest make sure to stop by the farm and say hello. To this I say—*oink, oink.*

But I digress.

For as I sit here attacking the keys of my word processor, I can see our mailman winding his way up the driveway, and in his hands are two large manila envelopes, both of which undoubtedly contain manuscripts which my wife and I, as well as an assorted number of friends and relatives, believe to be of sufficiently high quality to warrant publication. I meet him at the door.

"Well, it looks like someone's returning a few more of your stories, Mr. Soskill. Must get pretty frustrating getting all them rejection letters."

"Yeah, it is Mr. Barnum, but as long as a man has his health and family, well. What the hell, you know? A person can live with anything."

I must admit that I have a certain degree of hostility toward this man, who since I have known him always seems to have been the bearer of bad news. Somehow, unbeknownst to me, he has discovered the fact that I am a writer, and in all likelihood imagines that I am not a very good one, or why would all my manuscripts be returned to me?

I watch this aging servant of communication head across the street to a large white house which belongs to one William J. Mulvaney, who also happens to be a writer—but one who rarely gets rejection slips. Of course, this information has been volunteered to me by Mr. Barnum. Suddenly I decide that things have gone far enough. Isn't it sufficiently distressing that I must suffer the indignity of rejection almost daily? Why, on top of everything else, should the man who delivers my mail, a man who is prone to chattering idly, be allowed to harbor the impression (which, no doubt, he communicates to others) that I am something of an incompetent when it comes to the art of self-expression? So I act. Opening the door, I flag old Barnum down.

"Hey Barnum!"

"You call me, Mr. Soskill?"

"Yeah, come back here a minute."

And as the old fart trudges his way back up my driveway, I hurriedly open one of the manila envelopes he has handed to me, and observe that *The Magazine of the Christopher Marlowe Society* has returned to me *These Pipes Are Not for Smoking*, a short but pithy piece on crime in the sewers. Stuffing the rejection slip into my pocket, I hold out the manuscript to my mailman.

"Hey Barnum, I'd like you to read one of my stories."

"Well... heck, why would you want me to do something like that?"

"Look, you just take the story and read it and let me know what you think of it. Okay?"

I shove it into his hand. Reluctantly he takes the manuscript and deposits it inside his jacket. Although the bastard will probably fold, mutilate, and spindle my work, not to mention drip all varieties of liquids upon it, I really don't believe that having to type over an eleven-page manuscript is too great a price to pay to obtain the respect of one's mailman.

...

Old Barnum does not say much to me these days. It has now been two weeks since I handed him my manuscript. On Monday he nodded to me and on Wednesday when he saw me looking out of our bay window he winked. He gives no hint by the expression on his face whether or not he has read my manuscript, and if so what he thinks of it. I have decided that I will wait a total of four weeks before broaching the subject with him. This is the length of time one would expect to elapse before one would hear from any efficiently-run literary magazine that was the recipient of a relatively small number of submissions.

As I wait Barnum out, I sit at home during the day absorbed in my craft. Although my wife has suggested that I refrain from passing out any more manuscripts, I cannot help myself when the meter man visits us in the afternoon. His name is Austin and he is a gaunt-looking man with a long, greasy ponytail. On both of his arms as well as his neck there are numerous tattoos that appear quite stark against the pale tone of his skin. I have only met him once before today, yet that one time we exchanged words I came away with the impression he was moderately literate. So as he crouches in the basement reading our meter, I approach him.

"Austin, I was wondering if you could do me a favor?"

"Exactly what do you want, man?"

"Well, you see, I'm a writer, and I like to find out what all different kinds of people think of the stuff I write. So maybe you could take this story I've written with you and give it back to me the next time we see one another?"

By this time the two of us have climbed up the basement stairs and made our way to the front door. As the man looks at me with a somewhat puzzled expression on his face, I offer him a photocopy of *Spirochetes in the Springtime.*

"Why don't you take it?"

"Shit man, I ain't got no time to read your stuff!"

"Look, just take it and if you get a chance, look it over. I'd really appreciate it."

I stuff a fiver in his palm and suddenly he grabs the manuscript and without another word, the man walks off to his truck.

•••

One month after I handed Barnum my manuscript, I noticed that the man is no longer delivering our mail. It appears that he has been replaced by a young fellow who seems reluctant to engage in any sort of conversation. Nevertheless, when I asked him what had become of his predecessor, he told me that Barnum had retired. Understandably, for the past few days I have tried to obtain Barnum's home address. When I confronted the local postmaster and told him that I gave the now-defunct letter carrier one of my manuscripts, he looked at me in the most unusual way. All he would tell me was that it was against department regulations to divulge the whereabouts of any of its employees. He made it a point to say that perhaps if it were an emergency, he might make an exception, but in this instance obviously such a situation did not exist. I've come to suspect I really won't ever see my manuscript again.

•••

One afternoon more than four months after I gave Barnum my manuscript, I receive a communication from the man. It arrives in a

62

manila envelope with the copy of *These Pipes Are Not for Smoking* I had given him earlier. The communication is brief and consists of a message that is professionally printed on gray stationary, at the top of which are embossed Barnum's name and address. It reads:

Dear Bill,
THE ENCLOSED MANUSCRIPT HAS BEEN GIVEN THE MOST CAREFUL CONSIDERATION. UNFORTUNATELY, WE ARE UNABLE TO USE IT AT THIS TIME AND APOLOGIZE THAT THE VOLUME OF SUBMISSIONS PRECLUDES A MORE PERSONAL REPLY. WE HOPE THAT THIS WILL NOT DISCOURAGE YOU FROM SENDING US OTHER MATERIAL IN THE FUTURE.
Fiction Editor

Written at the bottom of this communication in a script I had seen many times on postage due envelopes is the message:

P.S.: Bill — In the future, make sure to include a SASE with all manuscripts — S.O.B.

•••

Probably because he is not due for at least six months, today the meter man sent his son over to return my manuscript. This child, who most definitely has the face of his father, can be no older than ten. As he hands me a copy of *Spirochetes in the Springtime* the boy says, "My daddy tells me to give you dis, and dat you should make all dem correcshuns he puts on each page. Den everything'll be all right."

I am shocked to discover throughout my manuscript numerous scribblings in red ink. Although these scribblings suggest some changes I am not in complete agreement with, I decide in view of the fact that this is the only constructive feedback I have received, I will take a chance and follow what undoubtedly is the advice of a twenty-eight-year-old meter man who never got beyond the eighth grade. As soon as I have edited the manuscript per his instructions, I will submit it to *Great American Fiction*.

···

This afternoon while browsing through some magazines at our local drugstore I happen to pick up the latest issue of *The New Yorker*, and notice that on page sixty-one, someone by the name of Stephen O. Barnum has published a fictional piece titled *These Pipes Are Not for Smoking*. On page four of the magazine, I observe a collection of pictures depicting all of the issue's contributors, and among them is a small black-and-white photograph of my ex-mailman. Adjacent to his picture is a brief biographical sketch that, among other things, documents his lack of previous literary accomplishment.

···

After weeks of frustration I have given up trying to convince certain people that I am the real author of *These Pipes Are Not for Smoking*. My wife too has accepted the futility of the situation, and suggests that rather than harboring any hostility, I should profit from the experience and act more prudently in all my future dealings with postal workers.

···

Today I received the following letter from *Great American Fiction*.

Dear Mr. Soskill,
I am pleased to inform you that our editorial staff has decided to publish your recent short story submission **Spirochetes in the Springtime**. *As per the standard policy of our magazine, you will be paid $500 for the manuscript. I would appreciate it if you would contact me immediately (please feel free to call collect) in order that we might expedite the details of this publication. Thank you.*

Sincerely,
Arthur T. Baron
Editor-in-Chief
Great American Fiction

...

This afternoon Austin came to read our meter and before he left, I handed him a check for $75. This was to reimburse him for the revisions he did on the *Infatuations of an Amnesiac Misanthrope*. I am proud to say that this particular manuscript, which his son returned to me last month, has already been accepted for publication in *Viewpoints*.

This man Austin never says much to me. Sometimes I find it difficult to reconcile his taciturn disposition with his obvious editorial skills. Yet in spite of the fact the two of us seem to lack a real rapport, I am more than satisfied with his work, and hope that the money I give him during each of our encounters will be sufficient to sustain his interest in my work. I have already paid the man a total of $245. This amount represents ten percent of my total sales to date.

Oh yes, before he left today I gave Austin a copy of *A Myopic Pope and His Struggles to Redistribute the Resources of an Alienated Isthmus Situated Somewhere South of the Milky Way*. I believe it to be a good story, yet for some reason unbeknownst to me, it always seems to have engendered the most negative of feelings among editors. Perhaps he will be able to identify the problem.

Seen It All

By Beth Gibbs

I knew the man was trouble the minute I laid eyes on him.

I walked into Mac's and there he was, sitting alone in a booth, magnetic, marvelous, and mysterious. The hair on the back of my neck stood up. He looked up and smiled. I took in his dark curly hair, bronze skin, chiseled features, and smokey hazel eyes. My heart beat faster.

I nodded to be polite and kept moving. I gave Mac a thumbs up as I passed the bar. I sat down at my table, crossed my legs and shot the handsome stranger a quick glance. We locked eyes. His stared at me with a look of hunger that had nothing to do with food.

He looked like a bad boy. I like bad boys. They don't ask for, or want, commitment. Neither do I. He picked up his drink, walked over and took the seat opposite me without ever taking his eyes from mine.

"Mind if I sit down?"

I shrugged. "Why ask? You already did."

He grinned. "Can I get you anything?"

"Nope. Mac's on it, but thanks."

Mac brought my order. I ate. The stranger drank and we exchanged pleasantries. Later we exchanged a whole lot more. By morning I was a goner, head over heels in *like* with the guy.

Love at first sight? Nope. Nada. That's for romantics. As a police detective, every drop of romance has been drained out of my body. I've seen it all. The dark side of humanity is a daily part of my professional existence. Murder, dismemberment, depravity, blood, and gore. You name it, I've seen it. So yes, all I admitted to myself, as I handed him a cup of coffee the next morning was, I'm head over heels in *like*.

He, on the other hand, looked at me like I was his breakfast plate of steak and eggs.

"What's your name?" he asked, taking a sip from his mug.

"Gladys. After Gladys Knight. My mom loved the Pips. She still misses Bubba."

He laughed.

"What's yours?"

"Larson, after no one in particular."

Larson was handsome, smooth, charming, and he knew exactly what to do with a woman's body in bed. I was looking forward to many more dates—and after date activities.

Yep, I was in *like* and smitten but, the little voice at the back of my head said: *girl, watch yo' back, yo' front, yo' top and yo' bottom.*

I ignored her and suggested that if he were available, we could get together on Saturday. I go after what I want, and I wanted Larson.

"Sure," he said smiling. "How about I make us lunch? I'm taking a cooking class."

He wants to cook for me! "Sounds great," I purred.

"It's our second date, then. Grab your phone. I'll give you my address and phone number. We can check in with each other on Friday to confirm. That okay with you?"

It was more than okay. When we kissed goodbye, he gave me a broad smile and a pat on my behind as he slid past me and out the door. Damn! The man was fine. He'd been a perfect gentleman and a perfect lover. Was I tripping? Were my bad boy days over? I told my little voice to be a good girl and chill out. She sucked her teeth and rolled her eyes.

Saturday found me at his place sitting on a kitchen stool drinking a glass of white wine and watching him chop parsley. He lived in an upscale gentrified renovated factory with seventeen-foot-high ceilings and twelve-foot windows facing the bay. Whatever he did for a living had set him up nicely.

I was impressed.

"So, what do you do to pay the bills?" he asked.

Uh oh, here it comes. If I tell him I'm a detective in San Francisco's homicide unit, he'll disappear as soon as he can into the fog of my history like so many others. I took a deep breath and told him. The knife in his hand stopped above the pile of parsley, pausing the rhythm of his chopping for a beat or two before finding its stride. "Well, that's interesting," was all he said.

Not sure if I should exhale yet, I asked him the same question.

"I'm a financial advisor, but I'm going to culinary school because I want to open a restaurant."

In my mind, culinary school was way more than a few flights up from a cooking class but who was I to complain? I was about to be on the receiving end of a wannabe chef's practice session. The results did not disappoint. He served me baked salmon and coconut rice with a green salad. It was nothing like my usual fare of fast food and takeout. Larson's lunch was as welcome as a hard rain after a California drought.

Afterward, I found myself on the receiving end of dessert in bed. My eyes were closed soaking in the pleasure of the moment when I heard him whisper, "honey."

I answered softly, "yes?"

He laughed and said, "no, open your eyes." I did and saw him holding a small honey bear bottle in his left hand. He grinned. "See? Honey."

"Oh."

Without a word, he drizzled a ring of honey around my left nipple and slowly licked it off. I groaned. This was new. No one had ever used my tits as a serving dish but if this was what he was into, he'd get no complaint from me. He drizzled another ring around my right breast, licked that off and then proceeded to drizzle a line from my breasts across my belly to my happy place, which got a lot happier after he finished me and the honey. Unbelievable!

That's how it went for the next several months. At my place we watched TV. I wanted to watch the basketball game, but he was into competitive cooking shows so I let him have the remote. Then it was pizza, beer, and sex. At his place it was gourmet meals followed by dessert in bed where chocolate syrup, strawberry jam, or whipped cream decorated the various parts of my body he wanted to sample. When I offered to return the favor, he said no. He considered serving me the only favor he needed or wanted.

Weird, said my little voice. *Shut up*, I replied.

Our dating pattern was predictable. The only real change came one night when he beckoned me over to my fridge, and listed the items he saw on the shelves: processed cheese, bacon, a half dozen eggs, a carton of spoiled milk and leftover Chinese takeout from Butterfly's, my go-to place, conveniently located between the police station and my apartment. Then looking pleadingly into my confused eyes, he talked earnestly about the importance of healthy eating and pointed out the absence of vegetables, which were clearly not taking up any space in my fridge.

Who was this man? I'll admit this scared me a little. It sounded like he was hinting long- term. I'm not good at long-term relationships. I've got a lot of baggage from two failed marriages and the disturbing nature of my job. And why would he care so much about someone like me? With his money, ambition, and class, a more polished version of womanhood seemed more like his type but he was directing all of his care, interest, time, and talent in my direction. Was Larson too good to be true?

Well, if something seems too good to be true, it probably is, said my little voice.

Stuff it, I replied.

70

Over the next few months, I shoved the little voice into a dark corner of my mind and allowed myself to relax into the rhythm of my growing relationship with Larson. I bought kale and carrots at Whole Foods and let him teach me how to cook the vegetables and serve them with poached chicken breasts in wine. I have to admit, it was good.

My refrigerator began to look more like his. I had more energy, and I was sleeping a full seven to eight hours a night. That was a big change from the three to five hours I'd been able to manage before Larson came into my life.

I was satisfied.

In spite of my satisfaction, my little voice kept sending up red flags and finally she screamed so loud, I had to acknowledge her concerns.

Why no arguments? She asked. *That's downright unnatural!* She was right. Up to this point there'd been none, and no guilt trips when my job meant canceled dates. This was unusual given my dating history.

And the food thing? Wake up!

He's going to open a restaurant, I told her. Honestly though, I did think it strange that we never ate out, went to the movies, or hung out at a club. He insisted on cooking for me at his place or teaching me to cook for him at mine. I didn't complain because my job was intense and by the end of the week I honestly wasn't interested in partying or hanging out. All I wanted was good food and great sex. I was getting both.

Finally, my little voice was tired of me ignoring Larson's growing obsession with me.

Girl, listen up! I know you think whatever this is is A-OK. But you need to open your eyes. Something ain't right. He totally controls the times you get together, what you do, what you eat, and what you do and don't do in bed. It. Ain't. Right!

I hated to admit it, but she was right. He was monitoring my food intake like a trainer getting me ready to run a 26-mile marathon, if running a marathon included gaining weight. I *had* put on a few pounds. Larson called it healthy weight and looked almost too pleased with my growing curves. "Plump and pretty," he'd say as he pinched my cheek and kissed my forehead.

As much as my stomach benefitted from his cooking and my pleasure centers benefitted from his habit of licking food off my body, it was beginning to creep me out big time. I mean, I understood the use of the sweet stuff, but now he'd moved on to sauces: béarnaise, peanut, and black bean. The most recent? Barbeque.

Because things were going so well, I'd resisted the urge to do a background check on him like I did on all the men I'd dated. But I'd reached the point where I could no longer ignore my little voice because in addition to her screams and warnings, my creep level had reached intruder alert.

"How about dinner out tomorrow?" Larson said after kissing me deeply and passionately at my front door later that evening.

Dinner out? That was new. "Sure, where?"

"La Scala, six o'clock. Can you make it?"

"Yes, but can you get reservations this late?" I asked. This was Friday, and Saturday all the restaurants in the city would be packed. La Scala was no exception. It was one of the city's *go-to* Michelin four-star restaurants. Reservations were as scarce as the Hope Diamond and about as expensive. I'd never eaten there—no surprise.

"I know the chef," he grinned mischievously as he left.

And I knew human nature. Something was up. I needed to know everything there was to know about this man. I couldn't wait any longer. I walked to my computer, whipped out my phone, and uploaded the picture I took of him as he lay sleeping in bed the morning after our first night together. I typed in his name and ran it through the national crime database at the FBI.

It took about three minutes and there he was. Looking as scrumptious in 2D as he did in three. He was honest about his first name—it was Larson, but there was a string of last names as long as my arm and as colorful as this year's Rose Bowl parade. I read his rap sheet and sat back in my chair. I took one deep breath and then another. Forget *like* turning into love. In that one instant *like* turned into loathing. The thought of our dinner date turned from steamy to stakeout in a nanosecond. I had work to do.

At six p.m. sharp the next evening I was at La Scala, seated at a table for two with a menu in hand that looked, well, interesting with items like:

PENNE PASTA WITH MEAT SAUCE OVER NOODLES

SIRLOIN STEAK WITH GARLIC, SAUTÉED ONIONS, AND WORCESTERSHIRE SAUCE

PIEROGIES FILLED WITH WILD MUSHROOMS AND LIVER

The chef's special of the day was MRS. LOVETT'S MEAT PIE in a puff pastry crust. I ordered three vegetable sides with rice.

"No entrée for you?" asked Larson.

"I've got to lose a few pounds. Healthy weight or not, my police uniform is starting to bulge at the seams." He looked disappointed as he cocked his head to one side like a puzzled puppy.

"Oh," was all he said. He shrugged and ordered the meat pie.

"Want to meet the chef?" he asked as the last bite of his meat pie disappeared behind two full lips. I tried not to think about where those lips had been last night, and what they'd been doing. I pushed those thoughts aside. It wasn't easy.

"Definitely," I replied. I put my fork down and stood up to take the hand he offered. We wove our way through the sea of diners to the kitchen. He pushed the door open to let me through. The door closed after him with a swish and a firm click. Locked.

"Mario, where are you, man? I want to introduce you to my girl-friend." Larson's hand was on the small of my back and I could feel its warmth penetrate my purple silk blouse and heat my entire body.

Mario emerged from the pantry. He was the spitting image of Chef Boyardee from the cans of spaghetti and meatballs I loved as a kid. He shook my hand, squeezed, and held it a few seconds longer than I was comfortable with. There was no one else in the kitchen. Larson's hand dropped lower to give my butt a quick squeeze. He smiled.

"So, Mario, what do you think?" Larson looked like the cat that caught the canary.

"Bellissimo! Bellisimo. She is perfetta, Larson. She is like an oven roasted beef sirloin, succulent and moist, braised slowly with onions and a delicious bone broth gravy." He kissed his fingers in that familiar Italian gesture. "Maybe we put her on tomorrow's menu, eh?"

In a flash I sent my left elbow to Larson's nuts while at the same time dropping Mario to the floor with a kick to his chest from my steel toed high-heeled boot. Before either of them could recover, I snatched my gun from its thigh holster, and told them they were under arrest.

The back door to the kitchen burst open. My team poured in, and while they handcuffed Larson and Mario and read them their rights, I yanked the wire out of my blouse. We walked them out through the dining room amid gasps and shocked looks. The team captain ordered the diners out and informed them that La Scala was closed—permanently.

I was appalled and disgusted by what the forensic team found. DNA from the slabs of meat in the freezer was eventually matched with several unsolved missing persons cases. Turned out that human flesh had been on the menu at La Scala from day one and the diners knew it. The police had to let them go because, in the US, there are no federal laws against cannibalism. The state laws that do exist prohibit obtaining and selling human body parts. I'll lay odds that the number of missing persons in the city will decrease by at least 50 percent over the next few weeks.

I was shocked by the fact that I might have been listed as one of them if the little voice in the back of my head had shut up like I'd asked her to. And I was royally pissed that I let my emotions fight with her and get in the way of my common sense. *So sorry*, I told her.

Just doing my job, she said.

As Larson was being pushed into the paddy wagon, he turned his head to look at me, sighed, and said, "Gladys, I'm so sorry things ended this way."

I looked at him and remembered his rap sheet. He'd been a person of interest in the disappearance of three women ten years ago and then spent three years in the slammer, convicted of trafficking in the sale and distribution of human body parts to a string of restaurants like La Scala in several other states. I wanted to curse and slam the door in his face but emotions are complicated things. I remembered our good times and replied grudgingly, "me too. I'm sorry too."

He grinned. "No, you misunderstand me. I meant, I'm sorry things ended this way because you would have been so good with roasted Brussels sprouts and a nice glass of Bordeaux." He slurped that famous Hannibal Lector sound at me from *The Silence of the Lambs* without shame.

I cursed him to hell and slammed the door in his face. And I thought I'd seen it all.

Betrayal
By Liz Bullard

The blind makes a squealing sound as the cord lowers it to the windowsill. The thud of its full extension solidifies that the day is over. Gathering discarded stuffed animals, tattered by warring and roughhousing twins, I am careful to avoid putting pressure on squeakers or pulling strings that prompt toys to talk. A block tumbles from my hand and into the toy box, louder than I would like. Shifting my eyes to the stairs, I strain my ears, listening for Zima and Zuma coming to investigate the noise. But the crashing block does not send them running. Perhaps this means I can have an evening snack and won't have to muffle the crinkle of the bag.

In the dining room, I gather scraps of paper from the cards the twins made in anticipation of their father's return. They are not used to his absence. This craft was supposed to quell their unease, and it did, though mine remains. My heart flutters when I think of Xion's return. I miss him more than when we were apart on missions in the past. How long has it been since we were in that world of deception and death?

Squeezing my eyes, I inhale and allow the scent of glue, burnt chicken nuggets, and the trash that should have been discarded last night to fill my nostrils. I am here, and far from the past. My husband, Xion, is not on a classified assignment, just away on a boys' trip with Maxi.

We are safe.

Slivers of the outside world seep in through the cracks, as rushing wind knocks against our home. I shiver and stuff my scrap-filled hands through the arms of a sweater I lift off the back of the chair.

The warmth from it eases the tension I feel and I wonder when discomfort became so foreign. Is this little life starting to feel normal?

Xion will be pleased. I smile and move the scraps to the bursting trash. Having straightened the dining room, I focus on my current distraction: the dishes. Putting the stopper in place and flipping on the water, I lean against the counter and imagine the sparkle in Xion's eyes and the shift of his beard as he delights at my revelation. What will he say when he finds out it took six years for this life to feel normal? This life came easy for him. Shedding our previous one like he was always destined to be a father navigating mundane difficulties. There are nights when he sleeps like the past never existed, as if we never hunted or killed for the agency. But now, maybe I will have more nights where I sleep like Xion. Days and nights where I do not fear the mundane being ripped from my fingers.

Chilling cold enters the house, and I turn around. Nothing. I listen, but no sound follows. My fingers twitch, but I no longer carry a weapon. The hairs on my body raise as if antenna searching for the source of fear that causes my heart to race. Water hits my finger and I remember I am safe. Turning off the faucet, I squeeze soap onto the rag, but must stop to grip the counter. My body shakes and I grasp the counter tighter until my fingers pulse. I try to slow the beating in my chest, but now it stirs an unease that almost makes me dizzy.

"Remember the mundane. Don't forget how wonderful it feels," I breathe, thinking back to moments before. To the dining room, filled with my children's crafts. To the moment where I sought the comfort of a sweater; Xion's sweater. I raise the collar of the wool-like material and inhale him. His warm scent, infused with the notes of brandy he enjoys, envelops me as I inhale deeply. I need his calm to cloak me like this sweater. And it does. It surrounds me as strong as his arms. I feel him holding me and his rough beard against my neck. A tear slips from my eye. "Do I really miss you this much?" I whisper.

That's when I hear a creak behind me. Calm fades and adrenaline surges as I turn to see that it is not my husband here with me.

A figure clad in black stands in the doorway between the back entrance and the kitchen. Baring my teeth, I step forward, eager to eliminate this presence from my house, protect my children. My body isn't used to these movements anymore. I am not as fast as I once was. My hands do not reach the assailant who swiftly sidesteps out of my grasp. An instant later, a throbbing fire radiates down my shoulder as his fist connects with my collarbone.

His fist?

Can I be sure it's a man?

My mind pulls in bits of information, but this puzzle has too many holes for me to see what is happening clearly. Yet I know this is a man.

I only catch glimpses of his eyes through the tight-fitting head covering. He keeps his movements quick, and it slows me down from piecing everything together. I stumble, almost hitting the ground. His hands grip my shoulders, and I am thrust back.

"Ah!" I cry out as my back hits the counter and ignites pain from an old battle wound. I bite down, almost drawing blood from my lip, praying my children's curiosity does not bring them to investigate the sounds.

The assailant watches as my chest heaves. Sweat curls the edges of my hair. He steps forward and my hand reaches for the soapy rag. My fingers, wet with pink bubbles, squeeze as I pour water and pomegranate-scented dish soap into his exposed eyes.

He yells and swipes at them. Unable to see, he skirts backwards into position, using the frame of the door to orient himself.

Glancing around the kitchen, I reach for pepper, the knives still too far out of reach. But this will do. This will keep him off balance enough to kick him out. Stepping toward the man with pepper in hand, I untwist the cap. The assailant hears my rushed steps and withdraws a blade from his belt. I step back as his reddened eyes try to make out my figure.

He steps forward, and I unleash the spice, throwing it at his eyes.

"Out of my house!" I growl as he thrashes against the fridge, knocking artwork and magnets to the floor. I want to use this opportunity to shove him away from the stairs, away from my children, but the pepper burns my eyes too and singes my nose, sending me into a fit of sneezes.

Pushing past the pain and watery eyes, I reach for the man, not fearing if I will grab an arm or the blade. But when I hear my son, time stops.

"Mommy, what are you doing?" calls Zuma.

My heart rattles faster as I hear the quick patter of his feet on the stairs.

With a brief glance at the assailant, I see a glint of glorified awareness in his red eyes.

He knows if he grabs my son, he has leverage over me. With a twist, the assailant darts down the hall. And then I know this man has been here before.

There are two ways to the stairs and this man just chose the quicker path. He knew exactly how to reach my children in our home. A space where only a handful of people have been welcomed.

• • •

The assailant will reach my child before me, but when I block him at the steps, I will not be empty-handed. Sprinting around the stove and through the dining room, I grab a colored pencil from the table.

"Mama!" my son cries.

I knew the man would have my child, but nothing prepared me for the sight of Zuma held against this masked man.

The assailant's arm is across my son's chest while his arms and legs flail. The man holds his hand to my son's throat. But his grip isn't tight. I know this because his grip does not cut off my child's cries for help. The man does not roughly thrash my son around, threatening to harm him. The blade is sheathed, back in place, and not pressed against my child's neck.

But the moon white scar on the man's wrist almost makes me drop to my knees. It is a scar I know well. I tended to it during our last mission as a trio; me, Xion, and . . .

"Maxi," I breathe, watching my husband's best friend hold my child hostage. My hand aches from how tightly my fingers grasp the pencil. My nails dig into my flesh. As I meet Maxi's eyes, I see the pain of what he has done, and it only makes me want to drive my weapon into his eyes.

He sets my son gently on the stairs, though he keeps his face from him. My son, whimpering and shaking, takes a step toward me, but this battle is far from over.

"Wait, my lovely boy. Go upstairs to your sister and lock the door. Mama will be there in a minute."

"Mama," Zuma whimpers, and I realize I never knew pain before this moment.

I swallow hard and try to hide the anger causing my body to shake. "Go, my love. I will be there soon. This is all just a silly game that has gone very wrong."

Sniffling, my son wipes his eyes, but obeys. He clings to the railing as he shuffles to the room he shares with his sister. It was only when I hear the click of the lock that I breathe. Glaring at Maxi, I say, "Maxwell, you will either die tonight or by some miracle, you will leave here with a limb or two."

Maxi's glistening eyes hold my angry stare as he reveals, "If you kill me, then both your family and I will die."

80

I linger on the last step, watching Maxwell. He sits at the dining table clutching a grooved glass next to my husband's brandy decanter. The way he sips from it, like this will be a friendly chat, makes me want to squeeze all the air from his lungs. But I need to be wise for my children upstairs. Glancing over my shoulder, I listen for the sound of their feet or rustling in their bed. Zuma had whimpered himself back to sleep as I rubbed his eyes and brushed away all his questions. Zima lay in her bed opposite him, never rousing from her peaceful slumber. Zima sleeps like her father, while every stirring sound rouses Zuma, like me.

Tucking away images of my children, I turn back toward Maxwell, who watches me now. I consider going back upstairs and grabbing the pencil I left on my children's dresser. The stairs creak as I sway, but I move forward toward Maxwell's assessing red eyes that have dulled to a pinkish hue. While his posture is that of a friend, I know all too well how quickly he can turn to foe. I take the chair opposite him. He reaches for the decanter and I snatch it back. "Do not touch what belongs to me."

Maxwell does not flinch at the warning in my words. "Key, I—"

"Do not be familiar with me. And I will not be familiar with you, Maxwell."

He grips his glass tighter and stares into the dark liquor. His lips move as he starts and stops his words. Once gathering himself, he says, "Kymora, I would have chosen another path if there was one."

"You wear betrayal so well," I growl.

The pinkish tone under his eyes darkens. I have wounded him. Good, I think as I watch the way he evaluates his next move. When he speaks, there is a depth of warning in his tone. He tries to keep it hidden, but I slip into my spy self, aware and assessing every word and every silence.

"And was leaving me to fend for myself in the agency not a betrayal?" he asks.

"That was survival."

"Then you understand my actions tonight more than you want to admit." His words linger as the house grows colder from another gust.

"Where is Xion?" I breathe, watching as he turns from me.

"These people know about our past, Key—I mean, Kymora," he corrects when he sees me about to interrupt him. Gulping from the glass, he continues. "They want us to be what we were, or nothing at all."

"You still have not answered my question. Where is Xion?" I repeat.

Maxwell brings the glass to his lips. I watch as his throat tightens and releases as the alcohol slides down. My skin prickles and fingers tighten as I restrain myself. His glass knocks against the table.

"Xion was all I had before you came along. I don't know if you ever grasped that. The tightness of our brotherhood. There wasn't a breath that we had that wasn't in sync. Then you came, like a fallen angel from the heavens."

I bang my hand against the table, shaking the scarce liquor that remains. Baring my teeth, eager to know the state of my husband and the reason for this deception, I say, "Maxwell, of course I know of your bond. Of your closeness. Our children would not refer to you as 'uncle' if that wasn't so. You wouldn't be aware of our new lives if you were not more than a friend. You are blood. Or at least you were."

I allow my last words to hang between us. To hurt. Though they do not inflict nearly the amount of pain I desire to unleash. Maxwell does not recoil at my strike. He continues retelling a tale I did not ask for.

"Kymora, you came as an enemy in more ways than one. As a spy on the other side of a war none of us knew we were fighting, and again as a foe to an end Xion and I were fighting for."

I scoff. "Are you referring to us abandoning the agency? Maxwell, there is no end to what we did other than death. We didn't want that, not for us, or our family."

"I was family," he growls.

The wind howls and the house rattles as both of us tense, waiting for the other to attack. But neither of us reaches for anything other than answers.

Maxwell expels a breath, then says, "I am family. Xion is my family. We wanted to create something different within the agency. Where death for a spy too old or too wounded was not the only option. But you took him away. You and your pregnancy changed him."

With each word, I see the venom fill his eyes. It is the same intensity that I saw standing in the kitchen fighting him off, my rag to his knife.

"Where is Xion?" I breathe these words like a warning.

"When you both left, I stayed. I tried to keep building a life within the agency, trying to dismantle it from the inside, but it's like a hydra, only growing more heads the more you cut off."

Maxwell grabs the glass, but it doesn't reach his lips. He grips it like a life preserver as he tries to keep his mind from slipping into whatever memory is tormenting his mind.

"Maxwell—" I begin, but then he speaks, as if narrating the horrors that continue to haunt him.

"You can't fight a hydra alone. You get consumed. Do you know what happens when a hydra consumes you, Kymora?" He pauses, though I don't think he is waiting for me to answer. I watch him as more of the scenes play in his mind, stirring tears too well. They do not fall, though the glistening is like a spotlight on his pain. "When a hydra consumes you," he continues, "you become one of the heads. You fight it at first. But then it is like a switch. One moment you are yourself and then suddenly, you are . . ." his words trail off and the knot in my stomach twists.

My throat tightens as my fingers brush over the drawing of our family on the table: Zima, Zuma, myself and . . .

"Xion isn't coming back." It is not a question, though the confirmation from Maxwell's fallen tear feels like a knife plunging in my gut.

The glass makes it to Maxwell's lips where he drains its remaining contents. When he slams it back down, its emptiness echoes against the walls that now feel so barren.

Maxwell's lips move, though his words come to me in a delay. "Xion had this way about him. This ability to not become whatever was surrounding him. He was supposed to be my cure, my salvation from this hydra. But he always chooses you."

Maxwell raises his eyes to me, and the pain is washed away by anger. Clenching the picture, I draw it to myself. The anguish I feel is one even tears cannot communicate. Everything is as broken as the children's artwork ripping apart in my fingers. I drag it from the table to my lap.

"Kymora, you can't be my hydra killer, but maybe you can be my redemption. I offer you the same choice I presented to Xion. He refused, and now he—"

I bring my eyes to his, halting his words. I don't want the confirmation to leave his mouth, not when my body is still reeling from his silent acknowledgement. Maxwell holds my gaze and continues. "The agency wants your children. Within them flows the blood of two of their best spies. If the agency can train them now, they will be unstoppable. I see glimmers of excellence in them. Especially when Zima—"

"Speak my children's names and I will cut out your tongue." The sweetness of my children's names is like a curse on his lips. It makes me grab the drawing clutched in my lap tighter.

"Kymora, I have done a terrible thing and I don't want to do any more terrible things. But I will if you refuse to bring the children to the agency. I must. But we can work together. We can kill the hydra from the inside. We can do what I couldn't. I can be whole again. Please, please, Key; do what Xion couldn't. Or I will have to kill you here tonight."

When I look at Maxwell, there is a pleading in his eyes. Like what he speaks is an offering that I should receive with open arms and a blessed heart. But now my anger is something more, it is resolve. It is just as much a weapon as the scissors I grip in my lap, under the drawing of my family. From my left hand, I allow the picture to fall and the scissors to remain in my lap. Gripping the handle tighter, I anticipate the way the blades will satisfy my rage as they break flesh.

I lock eyes with Maxwell's and allow my words to be salve to my wounded heart. "I will not take joy in your death. You meant too much to Xion for me to rejoice in that." I raise the scissors. "But know that with your death, there will not be another head sprung from this hydra."

Graduation Day

By Linda Strange

Nelida, Julinda's thirteen-year-old daughter, was home pregnant. The hot gymnasium would be too much for her. It made Nelida angry that she could no longer stand the heat, but Julinda had explained to her daughter that carrying a child did things to you, things you didn't necessarily like or expect.

The last time Julinda had been in this gym was two years before, on the day that Nelida had graduated. Dark brown water stains still swam like mysterious sea creatures across the ceiling. The same torn gym mats, plastic orange cones, and dented hula hoops lay jumbled under the tall windows. In front of the tattered blue curtains that hid a stage on which Julinda had never seen a performance, rows of chairs had been set out for the graduates. In front of these chairs were four more for the principal and the three fifth-grade teachers, a lectern with a microphone, and a table piled high with blue hardcover certificates.

Julinda and her sister Amalia were sitting in the parents' section facing the stage, near the back door where they knew the graduates would enter. It was Amalia's daughter, Gee, who would be graduating today, and Amalia wanted to get a good picture of her when she came in.

Julinda wasn't bothered by the heat, but the gym's strong smell of sweat, aftershave and mold did make her queasy. She couldn't be pregnant, but she remembered when she was: the shock of her body, her outrage at its unwillingness or inability to do what she wanted it to do. And she remembered what her mother had said to her on the phone last night. "Thank God you two aren't here, and I don't have to hear people say about Nelida what they said about you."

"Here," she'd said. Home. An island 3,400 miles away.

"Cape Verde," Julinda would explain when people asked where she was from. "Off the coast of West Africa. Where the hurricanes form before traveling across the Atlantic to America."

"Don't even bother," Baltasar, Julinda's contract husband told her. "The Americans don't know where anything is."

As Julinda took deep breaths to try to settle her stomach, a woman in a pink pantsuit and high white pumps sat down in front of them. She held an enormous balloon that bobbed above her head, completely obscuring the sisters' view of the stage.

Amalia and Julinda looked at each other.

"I'll talk to her," Amalia whispered.

"No," Julinda said, "I'll do it."

But just as she leaned forward to tell the woman that she needed to sit or tie her balloon somewhere else, Julinda caught sight of the vice principal, thin lips pursed, making her way toward them through the open gym doors. For a moment, Julinda panicked, then remembered that Nelida was no longer a student here and couldn't possibly be in danger of suspension.

The vice principal, her dress wet under her arms, stopped next to the woman in front of them. "I'm going to have to take your balloon."

"What?" The woman's gold hoops swung as she turned.

"I'm going to have to take your balloon," the vice principal repeated.

"Why?"

"Because they aren't allowed anymore."

"You gotta be kiddin'." The woman looked around the gym. "Everyone here has a balloon."

Earlier that morning, Julinda had arrived at Amalia's apartment holding two modest-sized balloons. "I forgot to tell you," Amalia had said, pointing to a rainbow-rimmed flyer stuck to her refrigerator door. "No balloons at graduation."

Julinda had felt her temper rise. It was the end of the month and buying a pair of balloons for her niece had used up the last of her cash.

"Why not?"

"They say it's a fire hazard."

"Well, that's ridiculous. I'm bringing them."

"They're just going to take them from you."

When they got to the school, however, no one did take them—as the woman with the enormous balloon had correctly pointed out, nearly every family had some. Though Julinda still tied her balloons to the bottom of her chair so no one would see. She blamed Amalia for making her feel timid. She blamed her for wanting to follow a stupid directive. She blamed her for outshining Julinda all those years ago when they were teenagers in Cape Verde, and for now in America, having raised a daughter who'd outshone Nelida.

Nelida had been failing almost everything when she graduated from fifth grade two years before. At the time, Julinda had been grateful that the school decided not to retain her ("with Nelida's poor attitude, another year in fifth wasn't going to be of benefit"), but upon reflection, she now thought that it might have been better if they'd kept her back.

Her daughter was home today lying under the fan, surly and miserable already. Julinda didn't want to think about what she'd be like when it came time for her to deliver in August.

She fished her phone out of her bag. Her husband was supposed to be in town this morning, down from Brockton to meet some of his pals. Baltasar was an older Cape Verdean gentleman, a nice widower three decades older than Julinda, whom she had married for the papers she needed to stay in America. They'd never once considered living together.

Amalia was also in the process of marrying to stay. Of course, for Amalia, it was more complicated. She had a husband to locate and divorce first. Julinda had never had a husband before America, a fact that her daughter never failed to mention whenever she railed at Nelida for getting pregnant at thirteen.

"I was *seventeen*," Julinda would inhale until she could feel the burn. "At least I finished *school*."

And what good had it done her? In Cape Verde, there were no jobs, and the only jobs she could get here were the kinds where one wasn't enough. She had three: a job at the Good Faith Eyelet Factory at the bottom of the hill, a cleaning job across town at Cherry Valley Supermarket, and some hours at The Lutheran Home one town over. That was the reason she was losing weight and coughing all the time. Her sister Amalia was wrong when she suggested it was because of the smoking.

Julinda watched her sister smile as she gazed around the gym. Amalia, a successful student, had always been happiest at school. While Julinda's school days, however, had been measured by the sharp slaps of the *palmatoria*, the blows of the paddle that other students were forced to give you in Cape Verde when you misbehaved.

She checked her texts. Nothing from Baltasar. Only a message from Nelida saying that they were out of ice cream.

Julinda could hear the graduates outside in the hall, giggling and whispering, waiting to enter the gym. They would come through the back door, make a sharp left under the basketball hoop in front of the kitchen, and then proceed up the aisle between the rows of parents' chairs.

The vice principal, who'd left in a huff, returned, her dress now sticking to her breasts. She was accompanied by a large man wearing a sweat-stained uniform with his name on it. When he bent down to talk to the woman in front of them, Julinda could see a thin sheen of moisture across his dark skin.

"We'll need to take that balloon from you, Ma'am."

The woman shook her head. "Nuh-uh. Everyone here have 'em, and I ain't giving mine up."

"You don't need to give nuthin' up." The man's voice was soothing, like water flowing over stone. "We'll keep it for you and give it back to you when the ceremony is over." His face wore a look of patience, not the pinched annoyance that had set the vice principal's features. "Because these folks sittin' behind you can't see." The man motioned at Julinda and Amalia.

"True that," Julinda said as the woman turned. She was enormous and could have struck Julinda's frail frame to the floor with one blow.

Amalia laid a hand on her sister's arm.

"Don't." Julinda flung it off. As if her younger sister had ever been able to restrain her.

The music began. It was the slow, solemn piece Julinda remembered. The woman in front of them handed the man her balloon as everyone swung around in their seats. Julinda saw Mrs. K., the ESL teacher, standing at the back door whispering into the ear of the first student.

"Gee will come soon," Amalia said as the chubby boy at the head of the line straightened, grinned, and stepped forward into the gym. "They do it by height, so the shorter ones are in front when they sing."

"I know how they do it," Julinda said. "We were here for Nelida, remember?"

Her daughter had been the last to emerge that day. Tall and long-legged, Nelida got her height from her father, a singer from Sâo Tiago who'd had eyes full of promises and a voice like honey. Julinda had met him only once when he came to Sâo Nicolau to sing *mornas* at a cousin's wedding. Nine months later, Nelida had been born feet first and howling. She'd been teased about her illegitimacy for the first eight years of her life in Cape Verde. It was only after they arrived in Waterbury that it became unremarkable.

The children emerged one by one into a gym transformed by anticipation. People leapt to their feet. Babies screamed as they were handed off to aunts, or to older sisters, or returned to their strollers, so their mothers and fathers could take pictures. Grandmothers and grandfathers struggled out of wheelchairs, balancing themselves on their canes. Tattooed men who'd arrived scowling cracked smiles, and then looked like they were going to cry. Cameras flashed everywhere as families pressed forward, consuming the space their children were trying to move through.

And then Gee was there, a small light-colored girl in a white ruffled dress, smiling with satisfaction. Amalia waved, took pictures, and then broke down sobbing. Mrs. K. leaned closer to Gee than she had to any other child. She spoke longer to her. What special advice was she giving to the student whom she'd taken under her wing?

The vice principal returned through the middle door of the gym, this time accompanied by two other teachers. They made their way to the central aisle, holding out their arms as they tried to get the parents to push back and give the graduates more room. A few people did take a polite step back, but most, as they jostled with one another to get a better view of their children, ignored the women.

Julinda felt sorry for the teachers. They were only doing their jobs, but she also understood the parents. They'd come to celebrate, to express their jubilation, to record this day against the future, because everyone in the gym knew that there were children in this line who wouldn't see another graduation, children who'd barely made it to this one.

"I'm gonna go back to school," Nelida said the day they got back from the doctor. "After the baby's born."

"How? We don't have the money for a sitter."

"Jose's family promised to give us money."

"They did? I didn't hear that promise."

The students continued to make their way through the shouts, the flashes, and the press of warm bodies, filing slowly into the rows of seats that had been set up at the front of the gym. Gee was already standing in the first row. The girl next to her had her arm around her. Someone behind her reached forward and patted her on the shoulder.

"She has friends," Amalia said, her voice filled with pride.

91

Nelida had had friends, but within a year of her graduation they'd been separated. Iris now attended State Street, the school where they sent students who wouldn't behave, and Waleska had been taken back to Santo Domingo because her mother was afraid that if she stayed, she'd get pregnant. As a result, Nelida spent all her free time with her boyfriend, Jose, driving with him and his brother in a yellow car with orange flames painted down the sides.

The processional had ended, but cries, shouts, and whistles of encouragement still ensued from every corner of the gym. The principal, Mrs. White, pink-cheeked and sweating, stepped forward and began tapping the microphone. "Could I have quiet, please?"

The three fifth-grade teachers took their places behind her, and Mrs. K. left the back doorway to stand near where Amalia and Julinda were sitting.

"We should have saved her a seat." Amalia waved to Mrs. K.

"She wouldn't have taken it. Not when there aren't enough seats for the parents."

Which was just as well because Julinda didn't feel like sitting next to Mrs. K. If Mrs. K. had done for Nelida what she'd done for Gee, Nelida might not be stuck at home today, nauseous, grumpy, and nursing the sores that had developed under her swollen breasts.

It was Mrs. K. who, when Gee announced last year that she wanted to be a model, had urged her to consider a more serious career. She'd taken her to the Metropolitan Museum in New York to see an exhibit about Coco Chanel. Gee had gone around for months afterward with the sketchbook that Mrs. K. bought her in the museum gift store, drawing page after page of evening dresses and mini-skirts for her first "collection."

"She ain't gonna be no designer," Nelida had said, but Julinda knew that Nelida also wanted to be a designer, or a model, or something that sounded glamorous, anything that might lift her free from the neighborhood.

Mrs. K. stood against the wall in front of a poster about drinking milk and next to a slender Hispanic man wearing a mechanic's uniform. Her face was flushed, and she'd pulled her blond hair up and twisted it into a knot at the back of her neck.

Mrs. White announced that before the certificates were handed out, the children were going to sing. The students rose, the music teacher stepped forward, and the parents held up their devices to record.

> *. . . I can fly higher than an eagle*
> *For you are the wind beneath my wings.*

Most of the women started to cry, Amalia included, but Julinda grew angry. Her daughter had ridden the winds, too soon and heedlessly, and she had the round belly and the bloated face to prove it.

Mrs. White tapped the microphone again.

"Because of the heat, I'm asking everyone to please hold their applause until all the students have received their certificates. It will make the ceremony go quicker."

But the parents did not want the ceremony to go quicker.

As the first student walked across the front of the gym, whistles and shouts of congratulation rose from a pocket of people standing at the back.

"Oye, Jaivan!" the man next to Mrs. K. yelled, pumping his fist in the air as the second boy started toward the podium.

After the third child was celebrated with a particularly prolonged tribute of shouts and applause, Mrs. White asked again, "please hold your applause until after all the children's names are called."

No one paid any attention.

When Gee's turn came, Amalia leapt to her feet and shouted like everyone else. Gee smiled and waved, and Mrs. K., who looked as teary-eyed as Amalia, lifted both her arms into the air as if Gee had come from behind to win a race.

By the time all the children had received their certificates, the gym was an even more pungent fog of sweat, aftershave, and perfume. Curiously, Julinda no longer felt nauseous. She felt better than she had all morning.

"We're going to give out the fifth-grade awards now," Mrs. White said.

Mr. Gonzalez, Gee's teacher, a bearded young man wearing a checked shirt and a crooked tie, stepped to the microphone. "There's only one student in my class who this award could go to. A girl who couldn't speak English three years ago, but who worked hard and never gave up."

A spontaneous chant of "Gee, Gee," rose from the students behind Mr. Gonzalez. Parents who didn't know Gee, but who had children who'd also struggled to learn English, or who'd struggled to learn English themselves, took up the chant as well.

Julinda felt the skin prickle at the back of her neck, and when Amalia laid her hand on her arm, this time Julinda didn't throw it off.

Mr. Gonzalez motioned for Gee to stand.

"Germana Francisca Silva."

Applause exploded like a great wave hitting the beach, and, for a moment, Julinda forgot her worries and thought of how proud their mother would be to see Gee selected for this American honor. She thought of their grandmother, who'd never learned to read, in her mountain village above the clouds.

Did one daughter's success have to be at the expense of the other? Until today, Julinda would have said yes. She might say yes again, but in that moment, as the cries of Gee's name set the balloons in the hot gym dancing, she saw the scene clearly before her. The geography of joy. The landscape of love and celebration. Julinda threw back her head as her eyes began to sting from pride as well as determination. Nelida would go back to school. Julinda and Amalia would make sure of it. She lifted her sister's hand from her arm and clasped it in her own.

Dessert

By Sam Keller

Chris arrives at the restaurant on time and her mother is already there. Always early, determined to occupy the seat facing the door as well as the moral high ground. Although Chris knows and expects this about her mother, a sour twist of annoyance rises in her throat and clenches her jaw.

She remains outside, watching her mother watch the door. The older woman is reliably dressed in her tweed coat and has had her hair done especially for their monthly luncheon. Although she holds the menu in front of her with her glasses perched towards the end of her nose, her eyes focus on the entrance. A hungry starling watching a grasshopper. No one in Chris's life awaits her presence with as much anticipation.

It repulses her. Both her mother's neediness and being the subject of her need. The familiar feeling of claustrophobia descends upon Chris. She looks up. Beyond the clay chimney pots and bare February trees, the sky offers a watery light. It's not a wide horizon, but enough to pull her from the crush of emotion she will not allow herself to feel. She can no longer be responsible for her mother's happiness.

Chris adjusts her handbag on her shoulder and scans the restaurant to ensure no one she knows is inside. Her mother believes they meet here because it's convenient—the restaurant is close to Victoria station where the train from Brighton arrives around sixty times a day—but truthfully, it's because it's far away from the theater where Chris works, her apartment, and any place she or the people she knows might frequent.

As she pushes through the front door her mother smiles and lifts her hand. A blue paper bag from The Bakery sits on the table.

Every month her mother texts Chris to say: "Your father wants to know if you'd like me to bring you anything." Her father's bakery is an institution in Brighton, where Chris grew up. He begins baking before dawn and works the till until closing time. Because her father always offers, Chris always asks for a pain aux raisins, and her mother always replies: "We'll do our best!" as if the offer did not come from them to begin with. As if her father did not have rows of pain aux raisins in the display case. As if Chris has asked her mother to make an unplanned trip to an impossible destination to retrieve a rare artifact.

Chris hangs her bag on the back of her chair and sets her phone on the table before she sits down. She acknowledges the bag from The Bakery with a light touch of her fingertips. The small blue shape squats between them like an accusation and an apology.

"How's Dad?"

Her mother knocks the question away with a flick of her hand and a short puff through her lips. The dismissal says all Chris needs to know; 'your father's mixing up sweet batter for everyone in our town but me. He has not been invited to lunch and does not deserve a moment of our time.'

"You decide what you're having?" Chris says as she scans the menu. The question is rhetorical. Her mother will order the French onion soup and a glass of house wine.

Her mother sets down the menu and removes her glasses from her nose. "How's the new script coming along?"

"Good," Chris gives a quick nod of her head but keeps the menu up between them. The play she is working on is about to go into production. Casting begins that afternoon.

"What's it about?"

"It's a horror. You wouldn't like it."

"Horror? What do you mean?"

Chris lowers the menu an inch to meet her mother's eye. "It's about a girl who gets sucked down a wormhole and finds herself in a universe made entirely of cake."

There's a pause as her mother searches Chris's eyes for sincerity.

"You're joking."

"Yes."

* * *

EXT. SUBURBAN GARDEN - DAY
CHRISTINE'S 6th birthday party. She is dressed as a ballerina. At the center of a decorated table is a tiered cake with a fondant ballerina on top. Children line up while FELICITY, 32, hands out triangles of birthday cake.

> FELICITY
> (Singing) Happy birthday to you. Happy birthday to you. Happy birthday, Christine. Happy birthday to you.

> CHRISTINE
> May I have the piece with the ballerina?

FELICITY blows up her cheeks to fatten her face.

> FELICITY
> Chubby ballerinas can't afford to eat cake.

* * *

Chris checks the time on her phone. "I have an appointment with the theater director this afternoon. I need to get going in about an hour." She looks around the restaurant and waves to the waiter.

"So soon? I wish you'd said."

"Sorry, it was very last minute," Chris says. "You know I have a lot on my plate."

"All work though."

Right on cue, her mother inserts Chris's lack of partner and family into the conversation.

"Yes, Mum. By choice, as you know."

"I do know. You're very important."

"Mum!"

"No, I mean it. You're a famous playwright."

"Hardly."

"All right then, well known," she air quotes. "Award-winning. Featured in *The Guardian*." She lifts her eyebrows, pleased to let Chris know she's seen the latest article in the paper. "Your father pinned it up in the shop."

"Oh, God."

"You should be proud. It's deserved." Her mother does jazz hands. "Except you're on the wrong side of the curtain, of course. You were such a natural on stage."

"I was never a natural, Mum." Chris jazz hands back. "You *hoped* I'd be. There's a difference."

"Pssht," Chris's statement gets the same hand-flick, puff-of-air dismissal the question about her father had received. "I only wish you'd told me that you were pressed for time, especially today."

Chris has no idea what her mother means by, *especially today*, and no desire to excavate meaning. Apart from their monthly lunches in London, Chris is sure nothing interesting or extraordinary happens in her mother's life. She catches the same train at the same time to the same place to order the same soup. *Especially today.* Chris refuses to give her the satisfaction of biting.

* * *

INT. LIVING ROOM IN A NEAT TERRACED COTTAGE IN
BRIGHTON — NIGHT
A lit Christmas tree stands in the corner. The TV
volume is down and Kylie Minogue's *I Should Be
So Lucky* plays in energetic silence. FELICITY,
35, enters with a vase of flowers she sets on
the coffee table. She lights the fire and moves
to the sofa to plump the cushions. CHRISTINE, 9,
enters. She is barefoot and wears a nightgown.

                  FELICITY
    You should be in bed.

                  CHRISTINE
    Not tired.

                  FELICITY
    Read your book.

CHRISTINE'S eyes are fixed on the music video.

                  CHRISTINE
    Who're the flowers for?

                  FELICITY
    Mind your beeswax.

FELICITY crosses to the television and turns
it off.

99

                    CHRISTINE
     Why?

                    FELICITY
     It's bedtime.

                    CHRISTINE
     Where's Daddy?

FELICITY steers CHRISTINE toward the door by
her shoulders.

                    FELICITY
     Finishing Christmas orders. Up you go.
     I'll bring you water.

                    CHRISTINE
     Milk please.

                    FELICITY
     No white food after six p.m., you know
     the rules.

They exit together.

                    * * *

    Her mother's hint sits between them on the table alongside the
blue bag, while the waiter takes their order. Chris orders a salad.
Felicity orders the French onion soup and a glass of white wine.
    Seeing her mother's look, Chris says, "I can't. I'm working."
    Felicity pinches her lips but does not make eye contact. "One
glass won't hurt."

                       100

Chris's phone buzzes on the table. "It's the director." She rises and takes the call outside. He's running late and they postpone their appointment to later that afternoon. When Chris returns to the table, her salad is waiting. Her mother is scooping the cheese and croutons out of her soup and piling the soggy, elastic mess on her side plate.

"Sorry, he was confirming the appointment."

The waiter has poured two glasses of wine. "I told you I didn't want—,"

Her mother interrupts by grabbing Chris's hand across the table. Her wedding ring digs into Chris's skin and her eyes flash with urgency.

"It's not my fault your father couldn't love me."

* * *

INT. LIVING ROOM IN TERRACED COTTAGE IN BRIGHTON-CONTINUOUS
The fire burns, the TV has been turned off. Christmas music plays on a record player. FELICITY, 35, enters and attends once more to the flowers and the cushions. There's a low knock on an outside door. She checks her face in a mirror and exits. A tall MAN, 37, enters the living room. FELICITY helps him with his coat. They stand very close.

MAN
I've missed you.

FELICITY presses her finger to his lips and points upstairs.

FELICITY
(mouthing) Christine.

101

The MAN takes his coat from FELICITY and tosses
it onto the sofa. They kiss deeply.

* * *

Chris snatches her hand away. "I'm not doing this now."

"There are things about your father . . ." Her mother remains forward in her seat. She watches Chris's fork travel from the salad to Chris's mouth and back. Apart from her excavation of calories, the onion soup sits untouched in front of her. "Things you *need* to understand."

"I don't *need* to do anything," Chris's voice carries a note of warning.

"Your father is not an honest person."

"That's not true, Mum."

"Well, he's not an honest husband then." She finally sits back in her seat, crossing her arms over her chest.

Chris imitates her mother's flick of the wrist to dismiss the conversation. Her parents married for tradition and convention at a time when people had few choices. She knows her father is neither a good husband, nor a very good father. He was never meant for those roles. He pours his love into baking. She forks a leaf and half a baby tomato into her mouth and chews for longer than necessary.

Her mother watches her like a sparrow might watch a cat. The cheese on her side plate has congealed and separated.

"Eat your soup," Chris says.

* * *

INT. A THEATER DRESSING ROOM, BACKSTAGE-NIGHT.
CHRISTINE, 12, stands in front of a mirror
ringed by light bulbs. She is dressed as the
Nurse from *Romeo and Juliet*. FELICITY, 38,
tucks CHRISTINE'S hair into a headdress. JOSIE,

102

12, enters wearing an Elizabethan dress and
gold headband.

                    JOSIE
        OMG, Chrissy, you look amazing.

                  CHRISTINE
        Same! Your dress is so pretty.

JOSIE spins.

                    JOSIE
        Thanks. Break a leg!

JOSIE exits.

                  FELICITY
        The thin girl always plays Juliet.

                    * * *

Chris finishes her salad and checks her phone, deliberately ignoring
her mother who is slouched in her chair, sulking. The waiter offers
them the dessert menu.

Chris shakes her head, "Just the bill please."

Felicity's soup remains untouched. The waiter begins to clear the
table. "Can I bring you something else?"

"No, thank you," Chris says.

Felicity sits forward and thrusts her hand out for the dessert
menu. "Actually, I'll have dessert. I can't travel home on an empty
stomach." She leans back in her chair, perusing the options. She reads
the descriptions aloud. "Cheesecake, baked, served with a selection of
berries. Homemade pecan nut pie with fresh whipped cream. Vanilla
bean ice cream and hot chocolate sauce . . ."

"Since when do you eat dessert, Mum?" Christine's stiff smile does not reach her eyes.

"Everyone needs a little bit of sweetness in their lives, Christine." Felicity smiles up at the waiter and orders two slices of cheesecake.

"Not for me," Chris shakes her head. "Just the bill."

"Two slices," Felicity repeats. "It's my birthday."

The waiter flicks his eyes from Felicity to Chris then to his notepad. He scribbles a quick note before heading to the kitchen.

Chris leans toward her mother and stage whispers with the energy of a shout, "what the fuck, Mum? Now they'll make a huge fuss and probably sing."

Felicity places her hand on her chest. "I deserve a treat."

"What do you mean? Is this why today is supposed to be special?"

Felicity looks pleased with herself. She slips her arms out of her coat and drapes it over the back of her chair. She's wearing a sage green dress that Chris has not seen before. She notices how it brings out the color of her mother's eyes. The care she's taken with her makeup. Her neatly manicured nails.

"Surely you're able to stay and celebrate your mother's birthday?"

"It's not your birthday, Mum."

"Well, they don't have to know," she gestures towards the kitchen, "and anyway, I do have a surprise."

Chris steels herself and takes the bait. "Something apart from your imaginary birthday?"

"Wait for dessert to arrive." Her mother rubs her hands together.

* * *

INT. BACKSTAGE AT A SCHOOL PRODUCTION OF
THE CRUCIBLE-NIGHT.

On a dark stage, CHRISTINE, 16, and JOSIE, 16,
dressed as Mary Warren and Abigail Williams,
peer through the curtains at the audience.

                    CHRISTINE
        I'm going to throw up.

                    JOSIE
        Why do you do this if you hate it
        so much?

                    CHRISTINE
        Mum says stage fright is a sign
        you care.

                    JOSIE
        Bollocks.

                    CHRISTINE
        She wishes I looked more like you.

                    JOSIE
        (American accent as Abigail) "But God
        made my face; you cannot want to tear
        my face. Envy is a deadly sin, Mary."
        (Normal voice) She's just jealous.

                    * * *

The waiter returns with two slices of cheesecake, topped with
thinly sliced strawberries, and drizzled with a raspberry coulis. A few
servers follow behind. Her mother's slice has a small candle burning
in its center. The staff clap and sing "Happy Birthday." When the
song ends, the waiter sets the bill at Chris's elbow. A few patrons

around them offer scattered applause. Her mother waves her thanks like she's taking a bow.

"Happy?" Chris asks.

Her mother blows out the candle and grins.

Chris sits back and regards her mother. A lonely woman who lives on an imaginary stage with no guiding script, no audience, no awards ceremony. She feels a moment of sadness. For her mother's dreams of acting, of fame and recognition, and how she has pressed her dreams onto her daughter.

Chris softens. "Okay, so what's the big news?"

Her mother's face lights up. "There's someone I'd like you to meet. His name is Derek."

Chris is immediately wary. Her mother has been known to dredge up old contacts from her brief stint in the theater, or worse, to try and set Chris up with someone.

"Mum, absolutely not, I'm not interested in meeting anyone."

"Derek's not for you," her mother laughs. "Derek's my boyfriend!" She speaks too loudly into the quiet restaurant, which attracts a few glances. Her mother giggles, thrilled with the scene she's creating. A teenager in the first blush of a crush.

Christine allows the amateur performance to settle and arranges her expression and her voice around the pitch of surprise. "Your what?" she says, while thinking, ah—so that's his name. She considers how she'll revise the script when she gets to the theater this afternoon.

The existence of a boyfriend in her mother's life is not a surprise to Chris. She remembers the tall visitor from her childhood who she glimpsed through the banister on the nights her father worked late. Nights when her mother made a special effort with flowers, her makeup, and her clothes. She remembers the music. The muted voices through the floorboards. Her mother's muffled laugh.

"Derek has been the sweetness I deserve, Christine." Her mother's tone challenges Chris to deny her this. She pushes the tines of the fork into the soft cake and licks them clean.

"You remember you have a husband?"

The same flick of her mother's wrist. "He has his own *interests*." Air quotes around interests.

Christine ignores what her mother is suggesting. "He's still my father."

"Little good that ever did you," Felicity says, but the animation has left her. She deflates and abandons the dessert fork on the plate with a clatter.

Chris glances towards the door. "You didn't invite him here today, did you?"

"It seemed like a good opportunity..."

"Mum! I can't meet your boyfriend like we're two friends sharing a secret." Chris drops her serviette onto the table. "I'm going to the ladies, and then I'm leaving." She tucks her credit card into the billfold, picks up her phone and pushes back her chair.

The bathroom is down a short passage at the back of the restaurant. The room is occupied so Chris leans against the wall. She texts her father—Thanks for the P aux R. You should come too next time—She's aware she's reaching out to him purely out of spite. A show of loyalty that excludes her mother. She watches the screen until it goes dark.

* * *

INT. KITCHEN IN A NEAT TERRACED COTTAGE
IN BRIGHTON-MORNING
CHRISTINE, 16, dressed in school uniform sits
alone at the table eating breakfast. Her FATHER

enters wearing his baker's jacket. His hands
are covered in flour.

                    FATHER
        Morning, Pet.

He kisses her forehead and sets a small blue
bag on the table.

        Your favorite.

FATHER exits.
FELICITY enters.

                    FELICITY
        Cereal again? We do have fruit you know.

FELICITY picks up the blue bag and drops it in
the rubbish bin. FELICITY exits.

                    *   *   *

Chris looks up and catches herself in a mirror. She realizes she
has worn her coat throughout the meal. An oversized, vintage trench
she can't button closed that gives her a retro 1950s movie actor vibe.
Her expensive haircut is cropped around her full, round face. She has
pretty eyes and a wide mouth, both expertly made up. Not beautiful,
she acknowledges, but attractive. She turns sideways in the mirror and
admires herself. Ample and approachable, she sees a creative woman
with a full life. Not a mean bird pecking at scraps. Her focus shifts
to the room reflected behind her.

Alone at their table, her mother keeps her hands in her lap but
hovers over the cheesecakes. Her eyes dart from the slice in front of
her to the one on Chris's side, like a heron watching frogs in a pond.

There's hunger in her stare, and rage, and when she abruptly reaches across the table and picks up Chris's cheesecake in her hand, Chris worries she might smash it into the tablecloth, or hurl it across the room. Instead, she takes a huge bite, then another; swallows without chewing, then takes another. Bits of cheesecake stick to her cheeks. Crumbs and strawberry slices drop onto the table. Red coulis smears her chin. She keeps on going, until she's eaten the entire slice.

Chris is rooted to the spot. She does not turn to face the room. She can't risk catching her mother's attention, but neither does she want to confirm what she is seeing. Watching her mother through the remove of the mirror's reflection, she can persuade herself she's watching a play. In that reflected theater, her mother exists in an imaginary dimension. The woman in the mirror licks her fingers and turns her attention to the second cheesecake still on the plate in front of her. She glances up once, then pecks and tears through the second slice. Too fast to swallow, too fast to chew, her lips curl around the dessert as if she resents every mouthful.

The lock on the bathroom door clicks. A young woman offers a quick apologetic knee-bend as she exits the ladies, but Chris ignores her. When her mother wipes her face with her serviette, Chris drags herself away and locks the door behind her. When she is finished, she stands in front of the basin washing her hands. She does not meet her own eyes in the bathroom mirror, afraid the illusion will crack and she will have to face reality. She focuses on her hands. Rubs them together, over and over, adding more soap and allowing the water to get hotter and hotter until they are red and raw.

When Chris returns to the table, everything has been cleared. Her mother's face and hands are pristine. Chris does not acknowledge the missing cheesecake. She signs the credit card slip, and slings her handbag over her shoulder. "Mum, are you all right?"

She smiles. "Of course I am."

Chris tucks the blue bag containing her father's pain aux raisins into her coat pocket. "Well, I'm off then."

"I'll stay for a bit."

As Chris reaches the door, a tall man approaches from outside. He holds the door open for her. She thanks him and they make eye contact. Derek is grayer than when she first saw him kissing her mother. He's grown a beard and wears glasses. Chris makes a mental note for the costume department.

* The End *

Sail On, Mom

By Kristina Giliberto

I wipe the outer lens dry and slowly scan the horizon. Even with binoculars, I can't see a thing that far across Nantucket Sound. I sit and wait as the gray, low-lying fog begins to burn off, leaving behind a haze that stretches out thin as a veil. I slowly inhale the salty, briny air of a moody Cape Cod morning, the kind that sits deep in the bones. Lowering the binoculars, my eyes continue to search the Sound from one end to the other. Its glassy water is reflective with memories, as it laps at dizzied footprints in the sand on shore.

I am certain they are coming. The chill that runs up and down my spine tells me so. My swirling thoughts settle, and I feel the warmth of the sun's rays as they begin to sparkle like glitter, bouncing across the sleepy waves.

Minutes pass. Or has it been hours? Days? Months? Time feels slow, then quick, then like nothing at all in this dream. I fight the urge to lie down and curl up into a ball, knees to chest, sinking into the sand as it wraps around me like a heavy weighted blanket.

Suddenly, or finally, off in the distance something flickers. My heart races as though it could propel forward. Once again, I adjust the outer lens from blurry to focused.

Just past Monomoy Island, I spot a flash of bright royal blue.

Not moving a single muscle, I hold my breath as if I were falling in an underwater free dive. Then, a flash of white.

It's been decades, but I would recognize those wide diagonal stripes from a million miles away. The sail of my grandfather's Sunfish.

It's them.

My grandparents.

They are crossing over to *this* side to get their daughter—my mother—Alison.

I don't yell out to alert Mom. The quiet is too sacred. My tense shoulders soften now that she has surrendered. Her back-and-forth pacing across the beach has left behind a jagged, serpentine path. So much struggle. Too much to bear, too much to witness.

She calmly sits at the far end of the jetty where it meets the low tide. Her legs dangle off a wide, flat rock with its smooth, water-worn edges. All ten toes are dipped in the chilly water.

When she stepped up onto the jetty, I watched as she first took all the time in the world and then hurried along like she was late to an appointment. Occasionally, she stopped to crouch down in between the jetty's perfectly aligned rocks, running her frail fingers across seaweed and barnacles clinging to their sides.

I imagined she was hunting for treasures to take with her. Stones, shells, her beloved sea glass. As a child, I spent hours exploring this very same jetty at Forest Beach in South Chatham.

My family holds a lifetime of memories along this scallop-edged stretch of coast with its salt marsh, bird estuary, and beach plum bushes. With sandy feet and sun-kissed faces, we would walk up the hill, then turn left down the secret path that led to the dirt road lined with cottages to my grandparents' house. They left us many years ago, but no doubt have been watching over all of us. I wonder if they knew their only daughter would be the first of their children to cross over. They loved each other deeply. She was with her parents during their final days, just as we have been by our mother's side for hers.

The sail is in full view now. Squinting, I can make out the tiny black speck of the infamous Sunfish symbol. I love that its creation was the simple outlining of a nickel with a fin, tail, and eye. Simplicity at its best. My wish for my mother is eternal simplicity. Freedom in her body. Ease in her mind.

Those sapphire blue eyes of hers occasionally look over to be certain we are still here, my brothers and I. We watch and wait while she watches and waits.

As the billowing sail gets closer, I can make out their silhouettes. I imagine Grandma wearing her skirted floral navy bathing suit with a terrycloth cover-up and a wide brim straw hat.

Grandpa has swim trunks, boat shoes, and a t-shirt with the words *Sail On* printed across the back.

The Sunfish approaches, then veers off to the left. Grandpa's engineering skills will make this pickup as precise as possible. He must be gauging the wind speed, rising tide, and anything else nautically necessary to safely get to his little girl.

He pulls the tiller to the sail, points straight into the wind, and slowly glides toward the jetty. I wish I could run over, be close one last time.

But it's just the three of them now.

I feel a gust of wind in my own sails from a lifetime of daughtering. The good, the bad, the right, the wrong. The emotional dance of mother and daughter. The wind pushes up and out of me . . . a swirl of release into the clearing, misty, moody air. As I draw a breath in, a tingle of salt and memory floods my senses, my body, and I feel transported to the first summer we went digging for sand dollars with my children, her grandchildren, on this very beach. Together. They were the thread that mended us.

Mom stands as Grandpa carefully quiets the boat to a stop. Then, nothing.

No sounds.

No movement.

Stillness.

I plant my feet in a wide, steady stance to anchor myself. Head tilted back, I lift my face toward the endless sky.

"It's okay, Mom," I whisper. "It's time to go. We love you."

She looks back at us and smiles, younger with her hair returned to its golden blonde shine. Then, she turns towards her parents and with outstretched arms falls forward until they catch her, pulling her onto the hull and into their arms.

Not to rush, but my grandparents surely need to get back to put out the clam dip, chips, and lawn chairs for cocktail hour. All their friends from the good ole days will be anxiously waiting to welcome my mother "home."

In a blink, the full November moon begins its ascent, floating over the Sound as the sun sets, painting the sky with hues of rose pink, deep ocean blue, and lavender purple.

It's true what some people who have experienced loss say. It begins and ends with love. A lot of beautiful and difficult stuff happens in the middle. But it's the beginning and the end that stay in the heart and soothe the soul.

I sink my tired, bare feet into the wet sand as the waves ebb and flow around them. There is peace in the dependable tide, rising high and low. I close my eyes and exhale. I can feel it now. I invite it in.

Between water and sky, between here and beyond, there they go. Wind in their hair, seabirds soaring above, we watch and wait until a flash of white, then a flash of blue disappears into the horizon.

Sail on, Mom.

Sail on.

Nonfiction

Introduction

There is no question that *flight* is the essence of the featured work within the nonfiction category of the 2024 Connecticut Literary Anthology. Whenever I've been entrusted to compile work—whether it be poetry or prose, for an online literary magazine, or for this cherished anthology of my home state—it appears to me that the chosen contributors have all telepathically communicated with one another beforehand to decide on the theme. It's a peculiar phenomenon that I wholeheartedly embrace—one that allows me to complete the puzzle of fractured pieces into an intact written canvas. The contributors have done all the heavy lifting, and I am just the privileged presenter.

According to the Britannica Dictionary, there are various definitions of flight: *the act of moving through the air, the act of flying, the act of running away in order to escape from danger.* This genre category begins with "Hunting Courage After Midnight," in which the narrator's quasi cat leaps into the air, and she must decide, rather soon, whether to rescue or leave it to the mercy of the Connecticut woods. The interiority and actions that follow show that this black cat symbolizes the leap of faith the narrator must confront within the midst of a profound life change. I envision the "Moms in a Parking Lot" flying in Escalades within the quiet streets of Greenwich before dawn, sacrificing much more than beauty sleep for their daughters. Dana McSwain's essay and Sharon Citrin Goldstein's speculative nonfiction piece encapsulate the dark definition of flight with narrators who run away from continued danger. There are two featured essays that allude to flight from the outset, such as "Flying Wheelchair" by Mary Keating and "Flying Fish" by Moriah Maresh. Beyond the resemblance in title, the topics diverge completely, except that they are both exemplary forms of writing. Within this larger theme, there are additional topics that shine. "One Cartwheel," "A Mini-Mental State Examination (MMSE)," "The Earring," and "Dave Has Wished Me a Happy Father's Day" all deal with facets of parenthood and caregiving in a myriad of wonderful ways.

Are you prepared to be in flight yet?

Yes, I have laughed and cried reading all the featured work, which is a testament of the fruitful and praiseworthy work that the Nutmeg State continues to churn out. With the help from Rachel Baila, who is completing her MFA at Fairfield University, I chose eleven pieces that moved and astonished me. I did not merely examine these pieces or collaborate with the wonderful contributors throughout the editing process. My stomach did leaps after a cartwheel gone wrong, I cupped my heart along the trails of backwoods, and I withstood the cold of rainy mornings. I did not read these pieces—I felt them in a visceral way.

May you take flight with each of them, and I hope you enjoy the journey as much as I did.

Victoria Buitron

Hunting Courage After Midnight

By Jillian Ross

How do you find a black cat in the dark?

One minute he was splayed warm across my lap purring as I sat out on the balcony watching random planes blink through stars and arguing with myself over the next day's impending appointment to get an experimental vaccine shot into my arm. I'm no wimp, but I did fear side effects. My finger hovered over the text chat, reluctant to press the "C" to confirm my intended compliance in the COVID database. A moth fluttered by. The cat's body tightened and quivered. I did not react quickly enough to suppress movement and—in one leap—the cat sailed over the balcony railing and dropped twenty feet to the ground.

I jumped up and peered over the railing down into the night. He was up on all fours, shaking his head. "Oh Fee, stay right there."

His narrowed eyes conveyed a cool disdain. He turned and sauntered toward the woods. Well, we call it the woods. But our woods isn't a piney mountain forest. It's a large swath of protected wetland. The high branches of its dying trees are strung together with wisteria gone wild. The patchy undergrowth of native brambles is crisscrossed with fallen limbs, and it is all anchored by a swamp of skunk cabbage. In the winter, the woods are just a jumble of charcoal grey scrawl, but spring greens it up nicely and fall is a golden showcase. The area is home to various species of wildlife, most of which are best viewed from a safe distance. Fee's potential foray into the woods would not end well.

I picked up my phone, then hesitated. So simple to just shrug and abandon Fee to his fate. I'm no wimp, but I'm no hero either. And I admit I cursed repeatedly as I tugged on my boots, grabbed my jacket and the can of cat treats, then raced downstairs and out into the dark to rescue the cat who is not mine.

Really, he's not my cat.

My Awful Wedded Husband brought the black furball home one cold December day and, with typical lack of imagination, named him Felix.

I call him Fee.

But this cat is no cartoon. He is FelixCityKitty, supposedly rescued from an empty flowerpot in the NYC theatre district. He is a bad-ass street cat—a slinky sleek panther with chartreuse eyes and a feral nature—a hunter. I limit his outdoor excursions to the balcony, but even there he finds victims. Yesterday he pounced on and then devoured a yellow jacket. Minutes later, the dismembered corpse came back up in a slime puddle of hairball and kibble. Last week, he captured a cicada. The thing was at least five inches long. Its papery wings fluttered in Fee's whiskers as the captor strutted victorious. I swatted Fee with the broom and, when the captive fell from his jaws, I swept the carcass off the balcony. Imagine emerging once every seventeen years only to be captured and dismembered by a feline predator.

Really, he's not my cat.

He is the abandoned pet of my Awful Wedded Husband. Really, what kind of man abandons his cat? Yeah, that kind.

On his Day of Departure—right at the start of COVID—AWH made two dozen trips down the stairs transferring all of his personal items to the van waiting in the driveway. I had Felix trapped in his travel crate right near the stairway, alongside a bag of FancyFeast, and a box of 99% dust-free CleanPaws litter. The bins of belongings I packed up for AWH went down the stairs followed by his leather

La-Z-Boy recliner and assorted kitchen items including the cheesecake pan, the burnished wood salad bowl mounted on a spinning disk, and various kitchen utensils that he'd flash like swords during his magic acts of food preparation. His cat and its accessories, however, were left behind.

I watched from the window as AWH sashayed down the sidewalk. It took me a minute to realize he wasn't coming back for his Felix. I couldn't even look at Fee as I unlatched his crate. He zoomed down the hall and sought refuge huddled beneath the teal blanket on my side of the bed as if he knew he, too, had been abandoned. For two months, Fee perched in the front window waiting for his owner to stroll up the walk and retrieve him. I couldn't figure out how to explain to him that maybe the girlfriend didn't like cats.

And so, Fee and I huddled together through the first year of COVID isolation. Fee scratched the furniture, and I scratched my head, contemplating Divorce in the Time of Corona.

Thirteen months later—legal proceedings at a crawl—I'm out here in the dark at the edge of the pond fumbling to access the flashlight on my phone and cajoling this crazy cat, "C'mon kitty, kitty. Fee, CityKitty, kitty..."

The pond, drained for a mitigation project, hosts a huge yellow excavator with a 45-foot boom. Dumped clumps of gunk form irregular islands around the metal monster. My light beam passed along its base catches a glint of gleaming eyes. Could be Fee—or could be the resident bobcat. I shudder. Perhaps a coyote? When I step out into the muck, my right foot sinks fast. When I lift my foot; my boot stays behind. I curse quietly then train my beam on the eyes, shake the can of treats. "C'mon kitty, kitty. Fee, CityKitty ..."

Those eyes—neon ovals in the dark—don't even flicker.

Really, he's not my cat.

My foot is freezing. I'm balanced in cold quicksand, and I really hope the snakes are sleeping.

120

The owl hoots from the pin oak. He's big and hungry, probably ready to swoop down and grab a midnight snack. Something rustles in the woods. Branches crack and snap. Black bears roam here. I shudder and step forward. The muck holds tight to my left boot—my foot slips out of the cozy sheepskin lining and now I'm barefoot, both of my Uggs held captive in the mud. I'm no wimp, but now I really do have cold feet. The open garage is likely filled with rabid racoons. The back door is open, too, and it is entirely possible that some nefarious soul now crouches in my kitchen brandishing my Cutco boning knife, ready to butcher me.

The oval orbs gleam steady.

"Fee," I whisper, shaking the can. The treats rattle their promise. I move forward through muck and murk, trying not to think about what my feet are stepping in. I click off the flashlight, squint into the dark. Moonlight glints off the reflectors around the cab of the excavator. I can just discern a small dark blob against the machine's tread. I'm no wimp, but I'm no superhero either, especially in the dark. "Fee!" I hiss his name and open the can of treats as I move closer, hoping the salmon aroma will not entice any other creature that might be lurking.

I stop several feet from him and bend down, shake a few treats into my palm, reach out. "C'mon kitty, kitty." His ears are flattened back. "CityKitty," I whisper. He inches toward me. "Good kitty."

His pink tongue makes contact with my palm. I grab him by the scruff. He writhes. I tuck him inside my jacket. His claws rake my neck and cheek. Clutching him close, I stagger back to the edge of the gunk, step onto solid ground, exhale a long sigh of relief.

"Fee, I saved you."

He hisses.

Really, he's not my cat.

I stumble and stub my toe on the concrete apron of the garage floor. My grip loosens. Fee thrashes. I grumble and grab him tighter. I should just let him go... devoting all this energy to saving an ungrateful creature makes no sense. I peer down into his little black furred face. His pink tongue flicks at my chin. My resolve crumbles.

Through the garage, I hit the button to close down the door, then wheeze my way up the stairs and into the kitchen. I scan the area. No intruders lurk, at least not right here. I kick the door closed, set the cat on the counter to inspect him for damages. I lift one paw. His fangs pierce my palm, and he launches himself through the kitchen, lands hard and zooms toward my bedroom. Mud streaks smear the hallway.

Really, he's not my cat.

And, honestly, I was WARNED!

I saved the video.

Fourteen years ago, the Justice of the Peace turned to me and asked, "Do you take this man to be your Awful Wedded Husband?"

I pierced the dead silence with a gasp.

"NO!"

He coughed, corrected the vow, and joined us in matrimony.

But the guy in the black robe was right the first time. I ignored the warning of the universe, though, and skipped right into the middle of the mistake. A Facebook meme explains the mystery.

Therapist: "Didn't you see all the red flags?"
Patient: "I thought it was a carnival."

I peel off my muddy jeans, wash my hands and feet in the kitchen sink. The scratches burn and bleed. I find Fee—a puddle of black velvet in the moonlight—curled on my bed inside my bathrobe. I should wash his feet, too, but they're tucked beneath him. I'm no wimp, but I'm not up to another round of claws and jaws. The bathroom mirror tells the tale. A trio of scratches runs from just below my eye, down my cheek and neck ending at my collarbone. Droplets of blood glisten like trail markers. My eyes widen. I tilt my head for a better look.

The scratches look like war paint. I touch one and flinch. I'm no wimp, but... I lift my chin... well, I'll be damned! I am a warrior! When I smile, the scratches crinkle. I dab at the damage with a warm washcloth, follow up with peroxide on a cotton ball. The scratches fizz white foam. And burn. I tug on sweatpants and socks, slip outside.

Back on the balcony, I pace and ponder. This cat is pure aggravation. For a moment, I want to pluck Fee out of my bathrobe nest and fling him into the night. A coyote howls. Clouds cross the moon. I... can't. I don't like him, but I cannot deliberately endanger him. Maybe a shelter? But the thought of FelixCityKitty huddled in a cement cage while no one ever comes to adopt him... no forever home... my vision blurs. I can't do it.

But really, he's not my cat.

I squint at the railing. I'm no wimp, but I've honed few skills with hammers and drills. Nevertheless, I will have to somehow fortify that railing to keep Fee safe within the limited outdoor environment available to him. I google containment options on my dying phone. Bird spikes discourage birds from landing on railings... hmmm, the sections of 6" plastic spikes resemble torture devices. And they're ugly. I scroll down the page. Harness and leash? No, he'd chew himself free. Or strangle. Of course, I could just open the back door and let him waltz into the world... a world filled with tiny ticks I don't want brought back inside to infect us with Lyme-Disease-causing spirochetes. COVID holds enough death potential. Not that cats get COVID... do they? But if COVID gets me, who gets Fee?

COVID. Right, my vaccine. I click on the appointment text and press "C." Tomorrow, I will show up at the appointed time, roll up my sleeve, and get the first jab to protect me. So I can protect Felix-CityKitty. We are, after all, stuck in this together.

Back inside, I approach the bed and find Fee is on my side. My side? I suppress a giggle. There are no sides anymore. The entire bed is mine. I crawl beneath the duvet and fall asleep to the rhythm of Fee's soft snore.

I wake to a soft pressure on my cheek. Fee's claws are retracted and the pads of his paw on my skin are soft as ripe raspberries. His wide eyes gleam amber in the morning sunlight. In the bathroom, I turn the faucet to trickle. He laps eagerly. The mirror tells me make-up is not an option, so I smear Neosporin across my face and down my neck with my pinkie finger. My mask will hide most of the damage. Fee hops off the vanity, struts down the hall and waits at the pantry door. I pour kibble into his bowl, refill his water, bend for my boots... ugh, my Uggs are still trapped in the muck. Flip-flops suffice.

At the security gate, I display my appointment text and am directed to the clinic location. The parking garage is packed. The long line of spaced-out vaccine recipients moves quickly through the clean, well-lighted space. Before I can even ask a question, the needle is in. And out. Quick. First shot done, one to go. I sit in the lobby for 30 minutes of observation because of my seafood allergy. I do not die.

I drive home slowly, calculating. Supposedly, side effects will appear in about six hours. I have plenty of time for Home Depot. I roam the orange aisles, mindful of directional arrows and six-foot distance requirements. I find nothing workable, but realize I do need, at least, measurements if I am to attempt to keep Fee safe.

This cat who is really not my cat.

Back home, the ache begins behind my knees. A fever simmers. I feed Fee a can of FancyFeast Flaked Tuna. The aroma lingers. My stomach rolls. I crawl onto the couch and pile on the blankets. Fee hops up, sits on my chest and proceeds to clean his paws. Fastidious Fee. What a good boy! I stroke his head. His tail thumps like a dog. He snuggles into my neck. I shiver, then roast. I'm no wimp, but the ache behind my knees has flared hot and seeped into every vertebra. I curl up and close my eyes. My brain burns. Fee purrs a soft soundtrack to fragmented fever-dreams. He perches on my shoulder and we sail across a blue sky on a cotton ball cloud. We stand firm on rolling seas. We climb mountains and achieve peaks formerly impossible to scale. We shrink into a lipid bubble motorboat and oversee the creation of a vast army trained to battle spiked invaders. We drift and wander through daffodil meadows. We glide on glass, carve perfect figure eights on the lake's silver surface. We spin iridescent on a whirling scrubbie and polish the tarnish from my golden years. I press my cold fingers into Fee's warm fur. His tail thumps. We are in this together.

Me and my cat.

Moms in a Parking Lot

By Laura Taylor White

Her headlights illuminate my foyer, waking the crystal chandelier. Rainbow dark dazzles as I wonder, am I still dreaming?

It's 3:05 a.m.

She is ten minutes early.

I fill two carafes full of fresh coffee, grab the Costco container of French Vanilla, two folding chairs, my daughter's dance school paperwork, and I'm out the door.

"Can you believe we're doing this?" she asks.

"I'm pretty sure we're already late," I say.

It's dark. The streets are empty. In Cos Cob, we see another black SUV turn onto Post Road.

"They're going there too," she states.

They are.

The courtyard in front of the dance studio is packed and the line is spilling into the parking lot. Two women are asleep against the locked glass doors of the studio in full sleeping bags with pillows. From their beds! Or maybe this is the "activity sign-up pillow and sleeping bag" they keep in the back of the Mercedes. Is that a thing? It probably should be. Either way, it's scary, yet inspiring.

Behind them, rows of silent parents, grandparents and hired help sit in lawn chairs and stare trance-like into the early air.

"I think we're 15th in line," she whispers. "That chick is sleeping!" I gasp.

"OMG, I need some French Vanilla," she giggles.

We are seriously the only ones in line who thought to bring coffee. The only thing keeping these other people awake is the fear that they might have to pee and then lose their place in line and their daughter will only get one of the six choices on their dance wish list for next year.

By 3:30 a.m., the line stretches through the parking lot. We wonder if our children are over-scheduled.

"Our parents never had to do this," I whisper, though our voices are highly caffeinated by now. Maybe they aren't whispers anymore. I offer the woman next to us a cup of coffee. She loves French Vanilla too. Who doesn't? She laughs. We love her.

"I feel like I should just sign her up for all four classes just so I don't have to do this again next year," my friend says.

"No way!" I am full-volume talking now. French vanilla wafts from my mouth with each belly laugh. "I'm so doing this again next year. I'll add classes one at a time. I may even just come back next Tuesday morning for the hell of it. This shit is insane. More coffee?"

The pee is somewhere up to my eyeballs. If it were light enough, the people around us would swear I was jaundiced. Nope, just urine in the whites of my eyes. I will absorb all the nutrients I can. I will stay here and laugh with my hilarious friend and our new partner in crime. I will drink more coffee. My daughter will get this class. OMG, what if she doesn't? What if my new friend just ahead of me gets the last spot? We should have gotten here at 2:00.

I am the worst mother ever!

People are double parked in all lots around us. We can't even see the end of the line.

A woman arrives at 4:15 a.m., clicking her illegally parked Cayenne locked with a beep so unexpected, the entirety of the line jumps.

"What the hell?" she says, and we tumble into one another trying to conceal our laughter.

We aren't laughing at her. We have just had too much coffee. Also, we are proud of ourselves for securing our daughters' futures on the stage. Broadway is calling. Their dreams will come true. Our dreams. We are the best mothers ever.

"More French vanilla?"

"Oh, yes please."

"May I have a cup of coffee?" asks a sleepy mother beside us.

"Yes," I reply. "For one hundred dollars... Baaaahhahhhahhh! Just kidding! Here's a cup!"

"Just pour it directly into my mouth," she yawns.

I consider this but pull another Yeti mug from my handbag.

"MORE FRENCH VANILLA!"

It's 4:27.

Now, it's raining.

My friend has a tarp in her car.

"Do you think I'll lose my place if I go get it?"

I am so full of piss and sweet, sweet stimulants at this point, I could bend a bitch in half with just my mind.

"I dare anyone to question your place in line," I say, just loud enough so that the mom pretending to doze in her husband's Everest sleeper opens her eyes wide.

She's to her trunk and back faster than most moms can wipe a green slimer from their toddler's upper lip. Let's not wonder why she has a tarp in her car.

This tarp is now touching my hair. The three of us huddle underneath the make-shift shelter's comforting crinkle—a tool I previously only believed known to landscapers, plastic with unknown last whereabouts shields us as rain plunks in heavy, unpredicted fist-sized drops.

"I am completely composed of urine," I confess between sips of coffee.

"I feel like I'm floating away," my friend agrees.

Our new friend leans in closer, the dry wrinkles of plastic dragging along her blond highlights as she whispers, "The woman in front of me seems... less awful. Maybe she would guard the tent if we let her in."

We elect the new girl as our representative. We can cross our legs to staunch the impending flow and shake in silent laughter, miracle tarp crackling around us.

"Pssst..."

The mark ignores our first attempt at contact, but to the two of us, the sound has signaled to our bladders to begin the evacuation process.

"Psssssssssst!"

The stranger turns, helplessly unscrunched eyebrows battle traction against fresh Botox under her damp and ruined day-old blow out.

"If we let you in," she nods to our coveted enclave, "would you hold our place while we go pee?"

Eyebrows soften relinquishing to the toxic brow of relief. We speak suburban forehead. She's down even though five seconds ago, she hated us, cursed the hot, laughter-soaked air seeping out from the edges of our asphalt oasis. I can hear her heart breaking from the purity of our revelatory gesture. We are heroes.

"If you hold it down while I go after?" our new ally replies. "Definitely!"

Our miracle sanctuary is the last holdout against the hurricane raging on hundreds of Greenwich's best mothers, housekeepers, and hourly-rate contractors. Our stronghold secure under the grateful watch of our newest friend, we dash into the storm hand-in-hand, our laughter the only thing between us and the incessant deluge as we scramble around the nearby dry cleaner's tall, white fence, drop our Lululemons around our ankles and challenge the sky to a pissing contest.

And we win.

We always win.

Spandex soaked through; we return victorious to our safe haven to another round of French Vanilla.

It's 5:32.

129

We are chilled-to-the-bone wet, but the tarp captures our heat and our coffee breath in a comforting cloud of new and forever friendship.

"Should we let others in?" I wonder.

I'm thinking of those women, curled alone in the faint stench of their lover's long-ago campfire sweat from a guy's weekend trip when he left her post-partum, all alone with three kids under three (and the night nurse) to cry as she rocked a colicky baby at 3 a.m.—the same child who she now again loses sleep and self-confidence for so that her daughter, her baby, can learn to count to eight wearing itchy tights that will have both mother and child melting into unrelenting sobs every Wednesday after peeling a wet Speedo from her tiny, exhausted body and throwing the worn water polo uniform atop the soiled soccer shorts where each item will do everything in its inanimate power to go missing between wash and dry cycles, cleaning crew folding, assigned location in child drawers and the big match this coming Sunday in Wallingford. Was she crying now tucked inside this alien version of polyester and REI taffeta, sleeping bag lips sealed tightly overhead, spiraled around the silent screaming deep in her uncaffeinated heart as un-peed regret sloshes against that heavy, throbbing, lonely lighthouse of love beating wildly beneath her recently augmented chest?

"Nah," our new recruit decides. "They're fine."

We laugh, checking our watches (5:45) and agree to meet one another more often, perhaps in this very parking lot so we can be together like we are right now.

"Let's camp out to buy tickets to the spring dance show."

"Front row, baby!"

We toast to friendship, vowing to purchase our own "sign-up tarps" for the trunks of every SUV we will ever own, and to register our daughters in ALL the classes so these losers in line behind us will be wet from the angry world pelting down on them from above and their failing urinary security all for nothing.

We now know we were all just six cups of coffee away from the women we were born to be.

Maybe we didn't beat the system, but for a few hours, hunched together in the security of this new world we created as our children slept, or maybe cried for us while our husbands fitfully slept through it all, those slumbering kings of Wall Street losing everything again and again in the stock market crashes of their elite nightmares, we were free.

Flying Wheelchair

By Mary Keating

At the end of July in 1998, hot, humid weather kept me inside for a week, saturating my lungs with stale air-conditioning. I needed a nature fix. Searching the web for a wooded park with easy trails, defined paths, and few hills, I found one in North Stamford that touted itself as an escape to commune with nature. "How perfect," I thought. "And it even might pass as wheelchair accessible." I phoned my friend Carol who agreed to meet me at the entrance around one o'clock.

When I arrived at the nature center, I realized I'd forgotten my emergency cellphone. "I'm sure I'll be alright," I thought.

Parked in the blue space reserved for wheelchair users, I got out of my Saab into my sports wheelchair. Even though I'm paralyzed from the chest down, it took me just a few minutes, having streamlined the process as long as strangers left me alone. Their unsolicited help usually involved inadvertently disassembling my chair or wedging it behind the passenger seat so I couldn't remove it when I got home. Fortunately, no misguided helpers were milling about that day.

While waiting for Carol, I studied the large map displayed behind plexiglass at the visitor's kiosk. I was happy to discover that a cross marked a help station at the opposite end of the parking lot and was about to check it out when Carol pulled up.

She jumped out of her car looking like an aerobics instructor. All those workouts with her new boyfriend paid off but couldn't increase her petite build. Regular swimming and pushing my chair around for years gave me a strong upper body. People always thought we were still in our twenties, though forty was no stranger to me, and Carol wasn't far behind. Proud of our fitness, we considered a challenging trail but finally decided to set off down the one marked "Easy."

Ten minutes later, traveling at a comfortable pace, we were already a quarter of the way down the first loop of the trail. We began to relax, taking in the cool breeze wafting through the emerald leaves. Cardinals and sparrows sang their symphonies to the oaks. I almost expected Bambi to walk out from behind the mountain laurel bushes while bluebirds decorated us with their flowers.

As we descended deeper into the woods, the trail slowly changed from hard-packed aggregate to hard-packed dirt. The woods narrowed. Thick tree roots crossed over the path now and then, but I managed to hop over them by popping wheelies. When a large flat boulder blocked our way, we reached an impasse.

"Where are those meddlesome helpers now?" I thought.

Just then, a young couple pushing a small child in a stroller emerged from the hidden trail beyond the boulder. I asked them if they thought it was okay for someone in a wheelchair to go where they just came from.

The father said, "Oh, yeah. It should be just fine. We didn't have any problems."

They easily carried their child over to us in his ten-pound stroller. I smiled at the infant as he reached his chubby hand out to grab the spokes of my chair's large wheels.

The couple chimed in together. "It's really a nice walk. We can help you over this rock.

We'd hate for you to have to miss it."

Safely over the barrier, Carol and I continued downhill. I knew there was no turning back but having a first aid station close by kept me from worrying too much.

Our journey continued just as the couple said. No major obstacles cropped up, and we fell back into a steady rhythm. Inhaling the earth laden air, we relaxed and resumed our conversation.

Our mood quickly shifted when the path turned and began to climb upward toward the parking lot. The incline loomed above us. Every foot or so along the way, thick tree roots caught my front wheels. Popping wheelies was too dangerous now because I'd easily flip over backward climbing such a sharp hill.

The woods closed in tighter as we ascended. The incline steepened. Slippery leaves coated the ground. Carol braced herself behind me as we struggled uphill only to slide back down the few inches we advanced. My shoulder and arm muscles burned. The harder we tried the more we risked careening downhill. A few times, Carol stopped my chair from somersaulting downhill with me in it. No help was in sight.

"So easy. You can do it in a baby stroller," kept repeating in my head.

"Okay. This is nuts," I said to Carol after several minutes. "Best you go to the help station. Bring back some strapping young lads to get me out of here. This is impossible, and I don't want to end up on the ground with you squished underneath me. Worse, you're gonna break your neck and end up in a chair too."

To the side of us, thin young birch trees formed a natural picket fence. We inched over to them, and I leaned against the saplings with my chair perpendicular to the slope. Even though the baby birches naturally prevented me from tumbling over, I hugged a few of them for extra support.

Carol was reluctant to leave me alone. I convinced her I'd be fine, trying not to reveal I was on the verge of a panic attack. After she disappeared up the precipitous climb to the parking lot, I alternated between praying for help and chastising myself.

I couldn't believe I'd been so stupid. I swore I'd never forget my phone again. And I would never again rely on complete strangers' assessment of accessibility. *What on Earth had I been thinking?*

Helpless and scared, I tried to fight the dread I'd never get out of these woods or worse, some nefarious person would find me. The minutes trickled into eternity. I grew more anxious. Overwhelmed, I promised God that if I got out of this mess, I would never do anything so idiotic again.

My thoughts veered into dark imagination as an eerie silence filled the ever-expanding forest. *Carol was taking too long, wasn't she? She must've fallen, or maybe got mugged. No that's ridiculous. Calm down. What if she did? I'll be sitting here forever. Bears and coyotes will find my corpse after the vultures mark its presence. Oh, God. Maybe they'll find me now. Are there bears in Stamford? Didn't someone just say they spotted a family in the woods up in Newtown. Newtown is far. Stop being silly. What's that rustling sound? A snake? By the time I realize one bit me, I'd be dead. What is that noise?*

Scanning the forest below me, a patch of red color grew at the bottom of the hill. Then a blue patch. Then blonde. The colors morphed into four young, strong-looking women hiking up the hill toward me. *Thank you, God!*

It occurred to me how I must have looked to them—a woman in a wheelchair perched in the middle of a steep hill, clutching a grove of trees, far from a paved trail. I started to laugh.

"Hey, I guess you're all wondering how I got here?" I yelled as they approached.

"Yeah, how the hell did you get here?" a stocky blonde in a red shirt, jeans and hiking boots asked.

"It's hard to say."

They gave me a quizzical look.

"I wanted to commune with nature for a while. I guess I got my wish!" I gestured at my predicament. "My friend's gone to get help."

"You don't have to wait around for help," the blonde replied. "Come on ladies."

Each woman grabbed a corner of my chair and flew me like a queen up to the parking lot.

As they landed me on the pavement, Carol appeared looking flustered. "Oh, thank God you got out!" she said.

"Why? What happened at the first aid station?" I asked, noting that only our two cars were in the lot.

"Mary, there isn't any help station here," Carol replied suppressing a laugh. "What's so funny?" I asked.

Carol didn't answer because she began laughing too hard.

"C'mon! Why are you laughing? I don't get it. The map clearly marked the help station with a cross. Why wasn't it there?"

"Mary, that cross wasn't for first aid," she managed to say between giggles. "Well, then what was it for?"

"A cemetery!"

Years later I still wonder where those four angels came from. I can't help but think that cross sent me help after all.

The Perfect Stranger

By Dana McSwain

We are in the woods. The new puppy races ahead, doubles back, attacks a tree. She shreds the leaves from a low-hanging branch with determination, as if they are responsible for some great insult. There's not much to her. She's all legs and ears and eyes and fury. She's terrible at walking. I never would have tolerated any of this from our other dogs, a lifetime of dogs all trained to heel, to stop it, to drop it. I no longer have the strength—or frankly the desire—to grip things tightly. I treat the new dog like an indulgent grandmother who lives far away and never has to deal with the consequences of her spoiling.

Branches snap around the bend—but close. The new dog streaks back to me, an ink blot puddling at my feet. There are bears in these woods, but it's not bears I worry about. They pay us no more than a passing glance before lumbering on, as uninterested in interaction as I am. Up trail, a woman appears and I instinctively relax. The men we encounter use clever devices to make themselves appear safe. Walking wide, nodding, calling a friendly hello, calculated kindnesses meant to reassure a woman walking alone in the deep woods with her dog. The trappings of courtesy, but what the watchers are really doing is granting me safe passage through their world, on their terms. *It's okay for you to walk in my woods. Don't worry, I won't assault you. Look how harmless I am.* Hate seems like a strong word. I'd like to tell you I choose my words carefully—I am a wordsmith after all—but the truth is I don't anymore. They fall out of me now, boulders down a hillside. I prefer the bears.

As she gets closer, I realize this woman isn't going to walk past with a nod. She's headed straight for me with a kind of intent that makes me break out into a cold sweat down the small of my back.

I don't know her, or for that matter anyone, here. It was one of the prerequisites of the move. Middle of nowhere, no neighbors, two bathrooms, thirty minutes from a Target, not a single soul for a thousand miles who knows me. No one to walk up to me at the grocery store and say, "Oh my God, I thought it was you," before picking up the reins of an unfinished conversation. No one to honk their horn at me and scream, "Call me, bitch, I miss youuuuuu," as they drive past. If someone knocks on my door, I have a baseball bat and a dog tucked behind my leg.

I study her as she crosses the last bit of distance between us. Small town haircut, the sort of rural mélange of clothing that could encompass outdoor work, grocery shopping, hiking, a local trick I've yet to learn. She's a perfect stranger. I assume her plan is to pet the puppy sitting quietly at my feet.

She's clever, this pup, nothing like the slobbering brothers that came before her. She will tolerate the stranger, a model of polite canine obedience, maybe offer a few cute tricks, allow her velvety ears to be admired. This perfect stranger might even, if the puppy is feeling benevolent, be offered a lick or a paw. My role in this bit of theater is to play the distraction with a carefully scripted narration. "Six months old. Oh, yes, she's very sweet. Smart? You bet. Smarter than me, that's for sure." The puppy will endure all of this, but I know she's just waiting for the stranger to leave so we can get on with the final act of this charade. The moment we are alone, the new dog will be overcome with conflicting emotions. First, she'll plead with me for help, and try to climb into my arms for protection. Terror will shift outward to rage as she tries to try to defend me from someone who is no longer there. Once she realizes we are alone and they aren't ever coming back, she will remember it's all my fault and attack me for letting someone so near us. No amount of "It's okay, you're safe" or "I'm sorry, I'm so sorry" or "Good girl, you're a good girl, baby," will help. The scene will play out until she exhausts both of us. I will end up in tears, wondering why I got a new dog after the old one died so suddenly, and how much of her trauma is my fault.

The stranger bends to pet two curly-haired ears framing a pair of narrowed obsidian eyes. "Can I tell you something?" It's more of a statement, her *something* tumbling out before I can reply. "I'm pregnant. I found out this morning."

My hands tighten on the leash as I search for the correct reply. The puppy has begun climbing her, scrambling at the woman's suddenly fragile-looking stomach, trying to wrap her gangly puppy arms around her waist. I jerk the leash to pull her down and earn a hurt look from those big, dark eyes. *Is this pregnancy a planned thing? A cry for help? Is she happy, sad, terrified? Or (d) all of the above?* I buy myself another moment with an apology for the dog's behavior. "Jesus, I'm sorry." Another jerk of the leash, another reproachful look. I regroup and settle for a caution. "How do you feel?"

The stranger shakes her head, frustrated as if I've missed the point. "Fine. I feel *fine*." She returns to the puppy, smiles at the lick on her ear. "For a lot of reasons, this is my last shot." Her voice drops to a hush. "I'm barely pregnant. It's only days. I can't...*won't*...tell anyone. Yet. I came here to be alone, but I saw you and I thought..."

Her unspoken words fall at my feet. I pick them up and read them like bones.

I thought I could tell a stranger, they say. *You're the perfect stranger.*

I roll the bones in the palm of my hand, consider the mercurial puppy now getting her belly scratched. Three wounded strangers, an unexpected circle of safety, deep in the woods, surrounded by bears.

I know this secret telling, this dark-matter web women weave, silken threads of secrets anchored in the hands of strangers. Under the fluorescent lights of public bathrooms, waiting rooms filled with outdated magazines *Slim Down for Summer, How to Spark His Attention After Baby, How to Be a Woman But Not That Kind of Woman,* in the pastel corral of the mammogram clinic, all of us topless and vulnerable, fear and secrets the low-fi melody that saturate every encounter we'll ever have. We learn the rhythm of sharing from our grandmothers, little girls collecting discarded shirt pin secrets from the dressing room floor, from words our mothers mouthed silently over our heads as we hid in clothing racks at the mall, a knitting circle that meets everywhere and nowhere, every day and never again, each dropped pin and secret knot creating a new pattern of invisible shrouds, swaddling veils.

"You don't have to explain." I drop the leash and kneel beside her. The puppy squirms under our hands in the moss, languid and ecstatic. "I understand."

And I wonder if that's why they hate us, those smiling men. Why they spend so much of their own lives trying to break us, attracted and antagonized by our capacity for pain; never learning that the tensile strength of a web lies in the distribution. That the sharing is what makes it possible to live as we do, surrounded by bears.

"I just I had to tell someone," she explains anyway. "And there you were."

Her face vanishes into the puppy's neck, the glimmer trailing in her wake whispers what she can't.

I had to tell someone.
I had to share this joy
This fear
This might be
Just in case

"Everything's going to be okay," I tell her. "You'll be a wonderful mother. You already are." I try to smile at her but she won't look at me.

"It's exhausting," she says, more to the dog than me. "The secrets we keep."

I can see the moment is wearing off; embarrassment and decorum are leaching through the fragile ritual that led her to me. I want to offer her something back to ease her discomfort, to balance the pattern.

140

For a brief moment, I consider sharing my own secret. I stand on the edge of it, open space all around me, measure the height of the fall. And I almost say it. I really do. I can even hear what it would sound like, what words I would choose.

"A watcher in the woods," I'd say, "found me. He wrenched my hands open, peeled my fingers away from everything that was precious to me. Some things fell to the ground and shattered. Others flew away. A few tried to crawl back to me, but I was so busy running, I left them there to die. And that's how you found me here. That's the only reason you found me here."

I weigh the balance of our secrets, taking into careful account the vulnerable set of her shoulders, the fragile weight of possibility inside her. There are other ways to achieve balance, ways to keep the pattern intact. Sometimes the only exchange needed is trust.

"I can keep your secret," I say instead, pulling her to her feet. And I find that I *can* keep her secret, and mine, too. One day, I'll do what she did: entrust my secret to a stranger. She'll be someone I don't expect: a cashier at Kohl's, an old lady on a park bench, even someone on the internet; a perfect stranger. I'll see her—know I can trust her. I'll ask her to take the threads escaping me and weave them into her own.

The woman finally meets my eyes, moves to go. I fix her face in my memory just in case I see her next year on the trail, sleeping child in a front pack, maybe a dog of her own racing ahead to greet mine. And if she's alone, her secret a possibility that ends with me here today, it will still live inside me. This perfect stranger won't be alone in the dimension that might-have-been. The threads that lead us here will always exist inside us both, deep in the woods. Infant, toddler, tween, teen, *mom I hate you, mom I'm sorry, mom I want to study abroad, mom we named her after you, mom please don't leave me, mommy I love you,* I'll guard her secret every day of my life.

She calls back over her shoulder.

"Bear season, you know. Be careful."

141

I'm afraid to look down at my dog; this is when things usually fall apart. A cold nose taps my hand and instead of terror and fury at everything she can't control, the puppy is straining at her leash, pulling me deeper into the woods, leading me on.

Dave Has Wished Me a Happy Father's Day

By Michael Todd Cohen

What's up little buddy?

And it was unclear if the neighbor, Dave, I think?, Dave—was talking to me or the dog and I dislike small talk generally, and general small talk completely, and I have tried recently to put an end to the performance of respectability and so I said, "We put in a new porch so now you're gonna have to deal with us out here." And when I walked away, I thought "deal with us?" What exactly did that mean, inflicting ourselves on the neighborhood like a wound? I do want that—to sting with queer joy.

Dave has wished me a happy Father's Day, and this, I think he must mean with respect to the dog, a chihuahua—who looked up at me, then, with goggle eyes and an exasperated grin begging to be wrestled into a baseball tee with matching hat—or as a general salutation to people who have or had fathers, which is everyone. Dave's hair is white and fresh cut. His Hawaiian shirt bulges bigger than mine. A watering hose hangs from his half-open hand like a careless cigar.

And I do want, after hearing it, and now that I have thought about it, for him to mean me, little buddy, because I humble this chihuahua in my shadow and because I had a father and now must stand on him to be my own and so it is sometimes good to feel little, which is different from small.

The Mystic Chords of Memory

By Elizabeth Hilts

The envelope was plain white, No. 10, a preprinted sticker with the return address, my name and address written in a vaguely familiar hybrid script-printing. The image of a Purple Heart punctuates the metered ink jet stamp from the post office of origin that urged me to "Just Dance." My husband asked, "Who do you know in Illinois?"

"No one," I said, though my family roots grew deep there. Then I remembered. "Oh, wait, it's that woman from ancestry.com."

In grad school I'd included in my memoir some stories about my ancestors, those who had come before me, those who had come together and lived and died and passed down genes and ideas. Those who made me. The writing was good enough, I was told, the writing was just fine. "But how can you call it nonfiction if you're making things up? Aren't you supposed to be writing about things that are true?" So I deleted the stories, focusing on the "truth" of my own remembered experiences.

Yet they haunted me, those stories; they wanted to be told, and I wanted to tell them. I needed to tell them. To justify my right to those stories, I started going on ancestry.com, following the leafy hints waving from the branches of my family tree, looking for facts to support the vague snippets of family history told over holiday dinners and in passing.

Finding my ancestors was like an elaborate game, gathering prizes hidden in census records, birth certificates, obituaries. Each time I got a hit that proved the family mythology I felt a little thrill, equal parts discovery and affirmation. "Oh, so that's true," I thought, once I'd linked from my father all the way back to the Mayflower and Peregrine White, the first Mayflower child born in the New World (a claim I'd always believed was wishful thinking on my mother's part). I was delighted when I followed a different branch of my father's family back and found Peregrine's brother, Resolved. What are the odds that those descendants would find one another generations and states removed from where those brothers built lives?

With each discovery I felt a sense of self; part of who I am is this—a descendant of hardy pilgrims, of pioneers, of people who gave up everything they knew in hope of finding what they needed, who moved ever west until one of them planted roots that grew deep in the fertile soil of Illinois. When I found an ancestor who had been born, raised, married, and buried in the Connecticut town where I grew up after my parents moved back east, I wondered if my father had somehow remembered this place he'd never been, if he had recognized it as a place that had once been home and that was how he'd chosen to raise us there.

My searching didn't dig too deep; I was, for the most part, content with having names and dates and places. I did do some cursory searches of obituaries looking for a record of the death of my mysterious grandfather, Noel. I cobbled together a few simple facts:

Noel, born July 10, 1897, died June 12, 1941. Son of. Husband of. Father of. Served in WWI.

I'd known a little more than this. My father had, of course, told a few stories about his father, my mother filled in some more, and I had drawn on those stories in trying to write my way to understanding my father a little better, in trying to write my way to understanding what happened between us. And so among those stories I'd included in my memoir there was this about the grandfather I'd never known.

My grandfather, Noel, used drinking to push away the darkness that came with the shell-shock WWI had bestowed upon him—a "cure" that cost him his wife, Alma, who divorced him and taken their boy "back to town," away from the family farm, making a scandal in their small Illinois community. If the boy snuck away to visit him, it cost him a beating. Yet Noel stayed on in the wide-hipped farmhouse where he had expected to build his own life on the foundation built by his parents and his grandparents. He'd tried, back in the early days of his marriage, to live in town, working in an office, but he was a farmer and he needed to be home.

That day when the chores were done something in the diminishing light stabbed into his wounded heart, flashed hard and fast against the tenderness in his mind, sparking tears and illuminating a single word: "Enough." He wiped his boots clean at the kitchen door, patted the dog's head, turned down the flame under the pot of stew. Then up one flight, past the bedroom he had shared with Alma. Past the room that still held evidence of the boy long gone (a cast metal Model T on a windowsill, the four hand-tinted paintings of nursery rhymes all in a row above the wood frame bed), the boy now forbidden to make the trip along the rough roads from town.

The late afternoon sun filled the western windows, dust motes thick as gnats as he walked down the hall past the rooms where his parents and maiden aunt had slept, past the rooms left empty for the brothers and sisters who never arrived for him or for the boy. The door to the attic opened into a blessed dimness, light from the fanlight at the front of the house not reaching all the way back there. He pulled the door shut behind him, slowly, carefully, crept up the stairs.

Was the rope already in the attic or did he carry it with him? It's likely that he had planned his suicide carefully; he was, after all, a farmer, a successful farmer, someone who must have approached certain tasks specifically, methodically. He would have looked over that rope when he chose it, made sure its *strands were not frayed, that it was up to the job. The rafter he'd have been sure of, trusting its sturdiness.*

Did he consider the seeds he was planting in his boy, my father? Did he understand that he was sowing an alien plant whose roots would spread, invisible, sending up new growth acres and acres—hundreds and hundreds of miles—away?

There are only two objects my father kept from the farm—a padlock, keys attached to the hasp with a thin wire circle, and a photo of my family homestead, where my grandfather lived and died. I don't know what purpose the padlock served but I can imagine my father pocketing it before he left that place that last time. The photograph of the house does speak to many rooms, of comfort and the expectation of large broods of children. But those rooms have never belonged to me. I have never been inside that house. I don't know their dimensions, their floors, their walls. I was not there when my grandfather climbed those stairs. Bereft of memory, I have only imagination. Since I do not "know" any of this, perhaps this would work somehow as fiction. Except...

When I logged on to ancestry.com one day I found a note from a woman in my father's hometown, asking me if I was related to Mary V. I responded that Mary was my great-great-great-grandmother. The next message was this: "I have a story for you, if you want it. Sincerely, N." Of course I wanted it. A few days later a copy of a newspaper article about Mary arrived in the mail. My husband and I had laughed about it, in part because of the flowery language used to describe how that three-greats-grandmother and her accomplices had gone to the hardware store to buy hatchets before descending on the Buena Vista Saloon one fine Bloomington afternoon. Men drinking away their families' well-being had fled in the face of the fury of those radical temperancists, the saloonkeeper—recognizing that he was outnumbered—perched on the bar and watched as the women shattered bottles, bludgeoned beer casks, chopped up the stools.

"When my dad told this story," I said to my husband, "the punchline was, 'And my great-great-grandfather wept.'"

Nancy had offered to send me other information about my Illinois ancestors. This seemed a remarkable generosity to me—she is not a relative, she has no vested interest in helping me learn about these people who are not her kin, yet she was willing to do research on my behalf. "Your family was kind of a big deal around here," she'd written. She'd mentioned something about newspaper articles about my two-great-grandfather's house and the farm that had been my great-great-grandparents', my great-grandparents', my grandfather Noel's, then my father's.

I reckoned these articles were in the envelope which I let be for a while, waiting until the early evening busyness of my own family made me a small space. My husband was in the kitchen clearing the counter so dinner could be made, my daughter was tending to my one-year-old grandson, my 17-year-old granddaughter was in her room on the phone with her boyfriend. I didn't take the envelope somewhere private to open it; I sat in the living room, lifted the edge of the flap, and ran my thumb along the adhesive strip. It opened easily and I pulled out a photocopy of a page in a newspaper. A headline in the middle of the second column was highlighted in yellow:

"N. J. H. Found Dead."

The tears come before I know they are forming, the grief so fresh and sharp it was as if I was learning for the first time that my grandfather had died. I sat down, hand over my mouth as if that would stop the eruption of sobs.

"Noel [middle name, last name], 44, was found dead a little after 6 p.m. (daylight) Friday at his home four miles southeast of [town].

Rudolph Luger, who operates the farm on which Mr. [last name] lived by himself, discovered the body hanging from the crossbeams of the attic.

Sheriff Walter Niemathehelmer and Coroner H. L. Lowell investigated and reported that he committed suicide. He had last been seen alive about 5 p.m. Thursday. He had been mowing the lawn at that time. It is thought he ended his life shortly after that."

He mowed the lawn. Shortly before the sun would have set in early June. There are some things I seem to have gotten wrong. The maiden aunt—Miss Almetta [last name], a name I first learned in this article, my great-grandmother's sister—lived in town with Noel's father, Sam, who'd been widowed five years earlier. I had not known my great-grandfather outlived his son. According to a map I found online, that house was just three blocks away from where my father lived with Alma and his maternal grandparents. The farm was so far out in the country I realize it's unlikely a small boy would have made that journey; perhaps the beatings my father endured were the result of his walking a few blocks to see his grandfather? I imagine him making his way over those three blocks, imagine him being greeted with a piece of cake and a tall glass of milk in the bright high-windowed kitchen, imagine him going back home and being told to go out to the yard for a switch. As a child my father had the same precious curls that have cropped up on my grandson's beloved head.

This, though, I got right. Fifty years after Noel mowed that lawn and climbed those stairs, the alien plant he sowed sprouted in a basement apartment in the Bronx. Late on an October afternoon my father called each one of his three children to say some things that had been left unsaid too long. He'd placed a list of instructions on the sideboard by the television. He'd had Jean, his long-time companion, lay out a new set of pale blue cotton pajamas and made her cover the couch with a plastic sheet. He'd had an extra dry martini with two olives in his Steuben glass.

149

Who knows why he picked that day? As the sun set, he swallowed the pills prescribed to keep him comfortable in that last stage of lung cancer, sent Jean into the kitchen with orders not to interfere, and lay back down on the couch.

It took a few hours, I'm sure. And I hope those heavy narcotics carried my father beyond the reach of the pain I cannot begin to imagine. He was already beyond the reach of fear. I had asked him a few weeks earlier if he was afraid of dying.

"Why would I be? It's just part of the continuum. You're born, you live, you die. No one gets out of life alive."

Had he always believed this? I wish I had thought to ask him how he had decided that idea. I wish I had thought to ask him how he'd come to peace with that idea.

I am, of course, hoping that he had come to peace, just as I hope that he slid out of this world on a dream. My father, beaten as a child, laid hand to me twice but he kept me at bay for most of our time together in this life. Now I understand: What else could be expected of one who had lost so much so early? What other lesson could that child have carried with him into life than this: "Don't care too much about those you love?" I understand: I am my father's daughter.

There are days, when a certain quality of light arrives just before sunset, when the sun weaves its rays through the trees, reflecting, refracting, setting just the edges of the leaves on fire, when I feel something sprouting inside me. Never at dusk. Never at night.

Never in winter, or spring; rarely in fall, though sometimes even then. I'll notice that particular beautiful light and hear my most private voice whisper, "Enough."

But, no. I cannot imagine what it would mean to not see that light, to not feel that vibration. I remember that what I need is not what my father needed, it is not what Noel needed. The familiar song vibrates, and I do take a strange kind of comfort in it but my heart insists, still, on remaining.

150

One Cartwheel

By Vesna Jaksic Lowe

One cartwheel led to a surgery, a screw in her arm, a cast, two slings, two braces, four months of physical therapy, dozens of x-rays, and another surgery to follow.

One cartwheel, on our front lawn. On the third day of third grade.

A type III medial epicondyle injury—meaning a bone in her elbow was pulled so far out of place, she needed an operation.

That summer and spring, she was cartwheeling everywhere. On the school playground. In front of the Washington Monument. On a bridge in Prague. I ordered her a pack of bike shorts to wear under dresses because she seemed to be in a permanent upside-down phase.

"Is she a gymnast?" people asked me.

"No, she just likes cartwheels," I'd say.

At the hospital, as antiseptic swirled with my anxiety, my husband asked if it mattered that she had been doing a lot of cartwheels.

"No, it only takes one wrong landing," the doctor said.

I wondered what the impact of that one wrong landing would be. If she will ever do another cartwheel. If I will go back to being the parent who always assumed everything would be fine. Or if I will keep seeing accidents everywhere, hear her scream every time I see another tumbling body.

After surgery, friends visited and asked how she was doing. They brought homemade cookies, balloons, books, sparkling journals, squishmallows—so many squishmallows. Then her cast was gone, and so was the sling, and soon the braces will be gone, too. The squishmallows stayed. The questions stopped.

Not for me.

I know the scar that snakes along her arm will fade, but what about the other scars? What happens when invisible wounds replace the visible ones? When the bodily gives away to the intellectual? I can handle the casts and the slings and the braces, but how do I brace myself for the mind gymnastics? Will I let her take risks with her body again? Will she let herself?

I think about where our fears and anxieties will land. If they will twirl in my head, tumble in her tween brain. Can one cartwheel change how I parent? I don't want to become a cast, restraining her movement.

...

When I was pregnant with her and gained little weight, people complimented me regularly. "You barely look pregnant!" they'd squeal, as if I were trying to hide that I was growing a human inside of me. I was eating healthy and exercising, so I felt deserving of some of that, but mostly, I felt awkward. My weight largely had to do with my genes and athletic background. It's also reflective of privilege—it takes time and resources to make fresh salads and go to prenatal yoga. And if we're complimenting pregnant women who gain a little weight, what about those who don't?

As my due date approached, the doctor told me I hadn't put on enough pounds. On one test, my baby measured in the bottom fifth percentile for weight. "You shouldn't be having a baby so small," she said. "She may not be getting enough nutrition."

It's best to get her out early, she said, and mentioned the possibility of a stillbirth. I left the appointment ridden with fear, and instructions to gain more weight and regularly check if my baby was moving. In between eating fried pork chops and guzzling GNC protein shakes, I laid on the floor of my apartment with my hand circling my stomach every few hours, then panicked whenever I didn't feel any movement.

I was induced early, so my March baby became a February baby—healthy and clocking in around 40th percentile for weight.

I quickly lost my pregnancy weight and the praises continued. "You look like you were never pregnant!" But nobody asked about the invisible toll—that I went into my induction wondering if my baby was fine; that I probably had post-partum depression but was too exhausted to deal with it; that my complications after giving birth included an ER visit. Behind my small, but visible belly, invisible scars had cut me.

Once my daughter was born, I never had to check if she was moving again. She scooted at 16 months, climbed structures for kids twice her age as a toddler, loved every sport she tried. Before she turned two, she fractured her wrist by catapulting out of her crib. At eight years came that one cartwheel.

...

Months after her elbow surgery, the doctor told me to push her stretches more so she could get her full range of motion back. It should hurt a little, he said. The rational part of me knew this was needed to loosen her tight ligaments. But when your child says "It hurts!" how do you keep inflicting pain? To stretch her muscles, I had to stretch beyond my comfort zone.

When that one cartwheel happened, we were lucky to be home, not traveling. To have insurance and live near a hospital. I'll take a broken elbow over a broken back or head, or a thousand things that could happen to an adventurous eight-year-old who can't sit still.

One moment, I felt grateful and lucky, the next I was sad and frustrated. What are the odds of this? Why her? Why now? One cartwheel exposed so many sides of parenting—fear and guilt fusing with stress and sadness, all wrapped in the intensity of a mother's love for her little one.

Months later, I still wonder—how could one cartwheel land us here?

Her body hanging in the air one minute, hugging a stuffy on a hospital bed the next. The thrill of being suspended in space in the morning, succumbing to anesthesia on the operating table in the afternoon. An arm free to explore and topple. A limb restrained by a cast, unmovable.

Parenting mirrors these extremes. When a scream follows a laugh, we shift from a steady routine to emergency mode. From holding her to handing her over to the doctors and nurses. Making jokes to make her laugh, then letting the tears flow once the operating room doors swing shut. Being her everything, then not being allowed in the same room.

I want to go back. I want to stop that one cartwheel before her arms touch the grass blades. I want a pause button for the moment she's still in the air, so I can warn her and grab her and protect her. I want to rewind time to that second before the landing.

But I am a parent, so I know better. Ceding control is parenting. Pain is parenting. Letting go is parenting.

One cartwheel, spinning towards uncertainty.

Flying Fish

By Moriah Maresh

I came across a writing prompt today: Write a letter to your younger self. What could I say to you, the little girl with pigtails and a red balloon, to curiosity embodied, equal parts anxious and awestruck?

I could tell you I remember, in flickering mosaics, the way it felt to be you. When you needed Mommy or Daddy in the room so you could drift off to sleep. When the Snow Fairies left gifts after the first snowfall of the year. When the woodsy swampland beside the house was "The Back of the Woods," where the White Witch dwelled, where you got your foot stuck beneath a root in the swamp, where you and your sister screamed until your dad trekked out in his work shoes to free you.

I suppose I could tell you to remember the canoe. It's long and bright, stored upside-down on two sawhorses, where the grass meets the woods, by the swing set.

Within that red cocoon, you have flown. Waves have lapped at your sides as wind whipped through your hair. Tucked in the middle with your sister, between your parents, who, like magic, row in perfect synchronicity, you have sprouted wings.

Remember how it feels to fly.

I know you. You want me to tell you more, to be more straight-forward. Evasion makes you anxious.

Perhaps you'd like me to offer tips. I could tell you to stay home from a sleepover, in case you wet the bed. I could also tell you to go to the sleepover, to trust the capacity of your bladder. I could tell you to say "yes" to that boy on the playground when he asks you out. I could also tell you to say "no." I could tell you to forget soccer in high school and move on to drama club instead. I could also tell you

155

to give soccer a try and switch to drama if you just don't want the field anymore. I could tell you every time going left will be a good decision, and I could tell you where I wish you had taken a U-turn, but knowing these things would change who we have become. And darling, we are dazzling.

I could tell you how your vial of innocence will crack, one vein at a time, how it will seep confidence and surety, until it ultimately crumbles. Know it happens slowly. Know that restraining emotions builds pressure. Know that saying "yes" when you want to say "no" obscures your view of you. Know that keeping peace at the cost of your individuality is, in fact, not keeping peace at all. Know that every child grows up, but don't be afraid to transform. Butterflies were once caterpillars. Yes, innocence crumbles, but you will create a kaleidoscope with those pieces.

People will tell you to aim for the moon, and you will do so.

I can tell you that you will quickly discover the moon is overpopulated. Instead, you will aim for comets and ride them beyond the moon. And when you whiz past the moon, people will be wishing on you. I could tell you where and when to aim your rockets, but I don't want to deny you the excitement of catching those rides on your own.

Just know, you stick many a landing.

I will tell you that some rockets explode and tumble into oceans. You will bob on the waves, dazed, and alone, but you are a strong swimmer.

I will tell you we always reach land, wringing sea water from our skirt and wiping mud from our boots.

There is that photo of us when we were two, lying on the sidewalk with our ear pressed to the ground. Do that more often. There is no such thing as silence. You will be surprised by what you hear when there is nothing to listen to.

You will be torn between the earth and sky, debating whether to swim or to fly.

Think back to the times when you and your father fished from that red canoe. Remember your sudden delight when a fish leapt from the water, those fish you wished to catch beneath the waves that flew above your hooks and bait.

Remember bobbing in that red canoe. Remember your joy at seeing another's flight.

And if anyone ever demands you choose between swimming or flight, remember the flying fish.

A Mini-Mental State Examination (MMSE)*

By Jeannine Graf

*The Mini-Mental State Examination (MMSE) is a 30-point question-naire that is used extensively in clinical and research settings to measure cognitive impairment. It is commonly used to screen for dementia.

Instructions: Ask the questions in the order listed.

Score one point for each correct response within each question or activity (Total possible points = 30).

"What is the year? Month? Date? Season? Day of the week?"
(5 points)

It is 2020 and my mother, Colleen Gloster Carolan, is about to celebrate her eightieth birthday. She calls to tell me she is preparing for her annual physical exam. "Fasting?" I ask.

"No, studying," Mom replies. "What do you mean by 'studying'?"

"For the cognitive test," she tells me.

"You're not supposed to study for a cognitive test," I say, "that defeats the purpose."

"If passing the test means I can keep my car keys, I'll damn well study!"

It's kind of a moot point, because we are in the midst of the Covid-borne state of national emergency and Mom's not driving anywhere. America is in lockdown, vaccines are not yet available, and her doctor's office isn't scheduling wellness visits.

Mom has "had it up to here" with the pandemic. "I'd rather die of Covid than of loneliness," she announces with Oscar-worthy flair. To her credit, she's been locked up alone in her New York apartment for four months and, all things considered, she's weathered it like a star. "Dammit," she says, "I just want to see my family. Is that too much to ask for my eightieth birthday?"

We, her family, debate this question in text threads that embroider a five-point star across a swath of shut-down states from New York to Indiana to Connecticut to California to New Jersey.

"What if I catch Covid on the plane and give it to Mom?" my sister texts from California.

"Then you probably shouldn't come," I text back from Connecticut.

The next text bubble: "If this ends up being her last birthday ever, I'll never forgive myself for not coming."

"Then you probably should come," I text back.

The story of 2020: afraid to be together, afraid not to be together.

In the end, eight out of twelve family members muster the courage to journey across the country's Covid-emptied highways and air space to gather in Connecticut for the summer birthday celebration on Friday, July 10, 2020.

We sit in the yard for the first hour, but the sun is beastly hot. "I'm more likely to die of heatstroke out here than Covid," Mom tells us. Then she puts on her facemask, picks up her wineglass, and heads inside.

We put our masks on and follow her into the air conditioning.

Her revised royal proclamation as she rips her mask off ten minutes later: "I'll die of suffocation in this thing!" This cracks the grandkids up; they've missed their spunky little Grammy.

"Take off your damn masks," Mom urges them as she sips her birthday chardonnay. "I can't understand a word you're saying under there."

But the family has agreed to a different indoor protocol, spelled out in no uncertain terms along those birthday-planning text threads. The kids glance toward me for permission to unhook their K-95s

159

from their ears, but I silently assure them with stern eyes and a head shake that the policy for the rest of us has not changed.

Sorry Grammy, my daughter tells her, we really can't.

Mom shrugs. "I guess nobody wants to be the one who kills Grammy," she jokes.

We laugh, but chardonnay and our family's shared sense of gallows humor can only relax us so far.

The pandemic has turned an eightieth birthday party into an illicit gathering. Like a gaggle of priests slinking out of a strip club at 3 a.m., the eight of us will take a vow of silence as we bid one another farewell and disperse guiltily back into our socially distanced lives.

Points: 5 out of 5

"Where are we now? State? County? Town/City? Hospital/Floor?" (5 points)

We are now back to when my mother announced in a phone call from Pearl River, New York that she is studying for her annual physical exam. Her primary caregiver, a physician's assistant named Patty, has tipped Mom off that the cognitive test she will undergo is called the Mini-Mental State Examination (MMSE). This has prompted Mom to search, download, and print a copy of the exam off the internet.

"Isn't that cheating?" I tease.

Certainly not, Mom corrects me, it's practicing. "Practicing is not cheating."

It occurs to me during our conversation that I might someday need to know Patty's last name. And the name of her medical group practice. And what Rockland County hospital Mom would want to be taken to in the event of an emergency.

But I don't ask my mother for this information tonight.

Tonight, all I want to commit to memory is her laughter on the phone when I tease her about cheating on the MMSE.

I want to marvel at her resourcefulness; not many people her age would even think to look for the cognitive test online.

Tonight, I want her to know that I idolize her for her spunk and her grace and her quick wit.

Points: <u>4 out of 5</u> *(What hospital?)*

The examiner names three unrelated objects clearly and slowly, then asks the patient to name all three of them. The patient's response is used for scoring. The examiner repeats them until patient learns all of them, if possible. **(3 points)**

FaceTime, YouTube, Facebook: three not-so-unrelated things. It's October 2020 and Mom and I are side-by-side, chatting through face masks on a drive down to the Jersey shore for an off-season escape to our family beach house. My eleven-year-old dog Shea naps in the back of the car. Except for the masks and the empty Garden State Parkway, this could almost be "normal times."

"Shea understands what it's like to be eighty," Mom says, glancing back at the fluffy sixty-five-pound golden retriever-chow mix dozing behind us. "She's an oldie-goldie too."

"You two do have a lot in common," I tell her. "People are always telling you how beautiful you are."

"Yeah, sure," says Mom, but I glance to my right and see she's grinning.

Just that morning as the three of us were leaving her apartment, a man had come off the elevator and greeted my mother with a hearty, "Hi there, gorgeous!"

I remind her of this.

She deftly deflects, "I think he was talking to Shea."

But a moment later, she becomes indignant. "That was very inappropriate of him," she decides. "Imagine if I went around greeting the men in my building with 'Hiya, handsome!'?"

I imagine it would put quite a spring into their orthopedic insoles, but I don't offer this opinion out loud.

Instead, I bring up her recent ophthalmologist appointment. "Twice," I tell her, "the doctor said there had to be a mistake on your chart because there's no way the beautiful woman in front of him could be eighty."

"Well, I don't care what anyone says about me *looking* my age," Mom insists. She raises her hands to demonstrate how her essential tremor causes them to involuntarily shake. "I *feel* my age with these awful, trembling hands and my creaky joints."

"And, I *act* my age," she finishes. "What person under the age of eighty watches informational videos about dementia on FaceTube?"

*Face*Tube?

"Wait, what?" I glance over to her. "*Where* do you watch them?"

Mom tries again. "The place online with videos..."

"*You*Tube?"

"Yes! YouTube! What did I just call it?"

I'm so full of laughter I can barely reply. "You called...it *FaceTube*!"

It feels good to be laughing hard together, side-by-side in our little Covid bubble on wheels. I dry the corners of my eyes, adjust my mask, and re-focus my attention on the road ahead.

"I confused it with Facebook," she explains when she's caught her breath. "Or maybe that damn FaceTime. The grandkids startle the hell out of me when they FaceTime me on my iPad while I'm reading."

As we approach the shore town exit, I lower the back windows an inch and the smell of the marsh's briny air floods the car. It rouses Shea, who lumbers unsteadily onto her shaggy paws and presses her wet brown nose against the draft. Mom is gazing out her side window, lost in thought. She shakes her head incredulously at the reflection in the glass.

"FaceTube."

Points: <u>3 out of 3</u> (*+1 bonus for coining FaceTube*)

162

"I would like you to count backward from 100 by sevens." (93, 86, 79, 72, 65,...) Stop after five answers." (5 points)

"I never expected to make it to eighty," Mom admits, warming her hands on a mug of Irish Breakfast tea and gazing out the sliding glass window toward the beach. Beyond the browning dune grasses, ripples undulate the fickle Atlantic Ocean's sun-dappled, peacock-blue surface. "It wasn't the family pattern."

Mom's father, Thomas Gloster, died at the age of seventy-two. Her mother, Eileen O'Connor Gloster, passed away at seventy-six. Out of her parents' combined nineteen siblings, only one made it to eighty.

"You and your two sisters have definitely bucked the trend," I say, curling up on the sectional sofa with my coffee cup. "Aunt Eileen almost made it to ninety, and if Aunt Maureen was a cat, by my calculations she'd still have about six of her nine lives left."

Born on Christmas Day 1932, Maureen Gloster Sullivan is eight years older than my mother. On more than one recent occasion, she has matter-of-factly declared that she has no idea why she's still here and she wishes she were dead.

What she lacks in *joie de vivre*, though, Aunt Maureen makes up for with a surplus of brain power. The "Gloster family google," her megabytes of memory are our go-to source for fact-checking names, dates, and family folklore.

What I wouldn't give for a thumb drive of that brain.

Prior to the pandemic, the Gloster sisters had a standing weekly lunch date on Fridays. Today, like every day for the past eight months, they check in with a five-minute afternoon phone call. As soon as she hangs up, Mom finds me in the kitchen.

"I mentioned the MMSE to your aunt on the phone just now. Of course, she knew of it."

"Knew of it? I'm surprised she hasn't had to take it."

"She did, a long time ago. Of course, she remembers all the questions."

"But does she remember all the answers?" I joke.

"She most certainly does," Mom replies. "She even taught me a trick for one. I told her I was nervous about having to count backwards from one hundred by sevens..."

"Hold on," I interrupt. "*That's* one of the questions? I couldn't do that without a pencil and a piece of paper."

"Well, your aunt can! She said, 'Oh Colleen, it's simple. You just subtract ten from the first number and then add three, and so on.'"

Mom watches as I stare absently at the seashell-patterned placemat in front of me, testing the equation hack in my head.

I can't believe it.

"Good Lord," I confirm, "it works!"

"Of course it does," Mom says proudly. "My sister has an amazing brain."

Points: <u>5 out of 5</u> *(Thanks to Aunt Maureen!)*

"Earlier I told you the names of three things. Can you tell me what those were?" (**3 points**)

Driving home from the Jersey shore, I ask my mother which other questions she's nervous about on the MMSE. She mentions one where the test-giver names three things and asks the patient to repeat them. Then, after moving on to a couple more exam questions, the test-giver asks the patient to recall the three things.

A question pops into my head: "Hey Mom, name the three online platforms we talked about on our way to the beach house."

Mom laughs first, then scolds, "Jeannine Marie, if this is your way of trying to trick me into saying FaceTube again, you can forget it!"

Points: <u>0 out of 3</u> (+1 bonus) *(At least I got her to say FaceTube.)*

Show the patient two simple objects, such as a wristwatch or pencil, and ask the patient to name them. **(2 points)**

"Name this," I instruct my mother, pointing to an object on her kitchen counter.

"This?" she answers, picking up the loaf of orange-cranberry bread. "If I had to name it, I'd call it 'An Occasion of Sin.' I shouldn't buy it, living alone. But I can't resist and they only sell it for a short time in the fall."

Now that I've shown interest in the bread, she's decided that I am both hungry and underweight. We sit at the table for buttered slices and tea, and I catch her noticing the swirl of silver with mother-of-pearl inlay on my right forefinger. "Do you remember this?"

"Your Aunt Eileen's ring," she replies.

Mary Eileen Gloster, who went by Eileen, spent her final years at Nyack Manor; the name evokes images of a patrician country estate on the banks of the Hudson River, but it's actually a rundown nursing home off Route 303.

Aunt Eileen referred to herself as a prisoner of Nyack Manor, never as a patient.

Despite her Parkinson's diagnosis, her speaking voice remained strong to the end and she used it to disparage the Manor's aides, management, food, and pretty much everything about the place. This did not incentivize the staff to do better by her, nor did it endear her to her fellow "inmates." But it did earn her a single room, because except for her devoted family, nobody wanted to be around her.

Wearing her ring reminds me of Aunt Eileen's extravagant personality and sense of style. In my childhood memories, she makes movie-star entrances to our family celebrations, decked out in oversized Chanel sunglasses, silk Hermès scarves, and three-inch high heel pumps.

She was forced to surrender her high heels for flats when the Parkinson's began affecting her gait, but even at Nyack Manor, my

165

aunt never gave up the scarves and sunglasses... and she always "had her face on."

To her younger sisters—who rarely if ever wore makeup—Aunt Eileen's daily application of foundation, eye makeup, and lipstick seemed frivolous and vain. But I thought her Estée Lauder cosmetics and high-fashion accessories brought a touch of Old Hollywood glamor to the otherwise drab facility.

One day when my mother was visiting Nyack Manor, Aunt Eileen leaned forward in her wheelchair and in a conspiratorial voice asked Mom to fetch a brow pencil from the cosmetics bag in the bathroom.

Mom grudgingly retrieved the overstuffed quilted-fabric bag, unzipped it, and plunged her hand inside to feel around for the brow pencil. Her fingers landed in a greasy, melty mess of a dozen or so foil-wrapped pats of room-temperature butter that had been crammed into the bag.

"Eileen! Someone stuffed butter in here!" she cried, showing her sister the mushed yellow mess all over her fingertips.

"That was me, Colleen," Eileen said nonchalantly. "Dig past that; the brow pencil is under there somewhere."

"Looking back, do you think hoarding butter in the makeup bag was a sign of dementia?" I ask Mom as we sip our tea and indulge in "An Occasion of Sin."

"Not at all," she says. "Eileen hated the margarine they served at the nursing home and complained enough that someone in the family began sneaking her pats of butter—I suspect it was your cousin Denise. Eileen stashed them away like contraband because she was convinced the Manor was full of thieves."

Points: 2 out of 2

"Repeat the phrase: 'No ifs, ands, or buts.'" (**1 point**)

I'm trying to understand why my mother thinks she needs to study for her upcoming MMSE cognitive test. Does she feel her memory fading? Is she worried? Should I be worried? On the phone I tell her, "You don't believe Aunt Eileen had dementia, and if anything, Aunt Maureen continues to show signs of cognitive *in*cline. If there's a genetic component to it, the Gloster sisters' gene pool is very strongly in your favor. Besides, I am a quarter-century younger, and I'm more forgetful than you are—no ifs, ands, or buts about it."

Mom is silent for a moment on the other end of the line. Then she asks, "Why did you just use that phrase?"

"What phrase?" My voice is all innocence, but I am grinning.

"You said 'no ifs, ands, or buts!' You looked up the MMSE online, didn't you?" she says, and I can tell by her voice that she's smiling too. "One of the exam questions is to repeat that phrase."

"And you just did," I reply, "so one more point for you!"

Points: <u>1 out of 1</u>

"Take the paper in your right hand, fold it in half, and put it on the floor." (The examiner gives the patient a piece of blank paper.) (**3 points**)

"If I bent over to put a folded piece of paper on the floor, I'd tumble ass over elbow and that would be the end of me," is Mom's reply when I ask if she has rehearsed this particular instruction.

Points: <u>1 out of 3</u> *(One point for knowing her limits.)*

"Please read this and do what it says." (Written instruction is "Close your eyes.") (**1 point**)

Now that Mom knows I'm familiar with the MMSE, I'm helping her study. But for this instruction, instead of "Close your eyes," my paper reads: "Tell me why you're worried."

"At my age, my biggest fear is not being able to live independently," Mom tells me. "Living in this fifty-five-and-over community, I've seen it happen to too many neighbors."

She thinks I can't relate to her fear of cognitive decline because of my age. I remind her that I am about to turn fifty-five.

"Well, I'm not talking about the younger residents," she clarifies. "I'm talking about the oldie-goldies like me. And like Mary Ann."

Mary Ann Ryan was Mom's best friend since childhood. Until her dementia diagnosis, she and my mother had lived parallel lives: born and raised in Yonkers, raised their families in Rockland County, widowed in their early seventies.

The day she got the call that her best friend was being moved to a memory care facility, Mom promised Mary Ann's daughter, "I'll go visit her as soon as she's settled."

But Mary Ann didn't settle. She was confused, disoriented, and prone to angry outbursts. The thought of seeing her lifelong best friend in this state terrified my mother. For a year, she made excuses not to visit. Then Covid hit and the excuse was ready-made.

It's one thing to read the numbers in the headlines, but quite another to see a loved one's face in the statistics. During the height of the pandemic, nearly one-third of coronavirus deaths in the U.S. were linked to nursing homes. Mary Ann died in June 2020, a month before my mother's eightieth birthday. It broke Mom's heart that she didn't visit her friend when she had the chance.

Points: 1 out of 1

"Make up and write a sentence about anything." (The sentence must contain a noun and a verb.) (1 point)

These are some of the sentences my mother has recently spoken to me, about dying: "**Am I** afraid of dying? I'm not. [pause] **I** honestly **believe** that."

"**I'm** not a big fan of pain, though. **Pain scares** me."

"**You** all **will be** fine without me."

"Let's face it, **I'm** a control freak. **I have** a long to-do list to take care of before I go."

Points: <u>1 out of 1</u>

"Please copy this picture." (The examiner gives the patient a blank piece of paper and asks him/her to draw the symbol below. All ten angles must be present and two must intersect. (**1 point**)

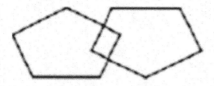

For the past five years, my mother has had an essential tremor that affects her hands and makes it impossible to hold a pen or pencil to paper with any steadiness. She struggles to sign her name to checks and greeting cards, and to fill out medical forms at doctors' offices. Once a gifted artist, she is unable to recreate this symbol. But this is due to physical—not cognitive—decline.

Points: <u>0 out of 1</u>

*FINAL TOTAL: **25 out of 30** (Our combined score on this creatively administered version of the MMSE appears to put my mother and me, together, in the "normal" cognition zone...for now.)*

Epilogue: By the time my mother finally sits for the MMSE, she is eighty-one years old and has been practicing the questions for a year. Patty, her physician's assistant, begins by asking Mom to name as many farm animals as she can think of.

"That's not one of the questions on the MMSE," my mother tells her. "Colleen, just name some farm animals for me, please."

Patty waits.

My mother sighs, then begins, "Pigs, cows, chickens, mice..." Patty interrupts, "Mice?"

"Have you ever even been on a farm, Patty?" my mother asks. Patty ends the exam there.

No need for further questions. My mother has passed.

The Earring

By David Capps

How such a simple thing could slip off her ear as she transplanted tulip bulbs, holding that mass together one year after the next, her kneeling form like my grandmother's, molded by Michigan summers.

How a little gem of cool could drop into topsoil, stardust blue, and be too small to notice, not by myself, nor my brother, after she enlisted us to help—and when it was over we dusted ourselves off, together.

How the years have made it as no one is: soiled, resplendent, fraught with a terrifying clarity you see in the sparkling eyes of the girl who begs from the median at the Trumbull exit to downtown New Haven.

Whether anyone found it—and observed at the heart of its incompleteness a sapphire star whose radial symmetry stemmed from my mother's hands—as she transplanted the same tulips, every time we moved.

Homecoming

By Sharon Citrin Goldstein

Kozienice, Poland 1945

Then, the Lord, your God, will bring back your exiles, and
He will have mercy upon you.

Deuteronomy 30:3

"Shmuel?"

He hardly recognized the sound of his name. It had been years
since a woman uttered it.

Shmuel Goldstein returned to his hometown of Kozienice clad
in a Russian uniform two months before the end of World War II.
His escape had been risky, but worth the gamble.

Earlier that winter, his battalion had entered Germany by force
and was in position for victory a mere sixty kilometers from the German capital of Berlin. But when charging uphill from the frontline,
a German sniper blasted Shmuel's calf. Bleeding and delirious, he
was evacuated with other casualties to a hospital in Poznan, Poland.
From there, desperation and opportunity guided his next move.
After fighting for his family, his home, and his life, the prospect of
freedom and the chance to reunite with his family could be close at
hand. With two boards as crutches, he hobbled toward the station
and hopped a train headed homeward to Kozienice.

Shmuel arrived wounded and weary and without high expectations. "I heard already what was done to the Jews," he later wrote.

"I met an empty city. I walked the streets where Jews used to
live. Yes, the streets were there, the sidewalk was there, but no Jews.
I walked on the sidewalk alone and remembered who used to live

172

in every place I passed but nobody was there anymore. The Jewish houses were burned out, empty fields. Only a few brick houses were left and Polish families lived there."

Others like him began to turn up, each with the hope of finding somebody alive. "But hardly anybody survived," he noted. "We started to ask one another if they knew anyone from our family. And nobody in my family survived."

That was how he learned with certainty of his family's fate. His father and a sister with her husband and two children perished in the gas chambers of Treblinka. Another sister tried to escape and was shot in the forest. One of his brothers moved to the town of Lodz and disappeared together with his wife and six children. One more sister and a second brother along with his wife and three children died from hunger. The same sister had a seven-year-old boy who was sent with a group of children to the munitions labor camp at Skarzysko-Kamienna where they served as targets for Dumdum bullet experiments. Coldblooded Nazi doctors examined the damage the exploded bullets caused to the youngsters' little bodies.

"We [the survivors] remained orphaned and were afraid to remain alone," Shmuel wrote. "Every one of us had a terrible story to tell, an unbelievable story. We were afraid, we were not used to be free, to see the blue sky. We were worried about tomorrow, where should we go, what are we going to live from."

Two sisters Sabina and Genya, their best friend Pola, and her seven-year-old daughter Ruth in tow also returned to Kozienice that winter. Having trudged for two-and-a-half weeks through deep snow in subzero temperatures, Sabina's toes had numbed from frost, her legs were severely swollen, and half her body was covered with sores. It didn't help that her leather shoes—worn through two grueling years in forced labor camps—were frayed and falling apart. Poor little Ruth. Since outgrowing her tot-sized shoes, her feet were wrapped in rags. Whenever snowfall in the camps smushed into a grey slippery sludge, Pola hung the schmattes to dry overnight and exhaled her warm breath on Ruth's feet.

Once outside the camp, Sabina noted how the snowbanks glistened frosty white. She shivered. An icy wind ripped through her only dress. The back of the dress had been smeared with red paint for the winter; in the summers, the color changed to white. To "pretty up" her appearance in the camps, she had trimmed the dress with fabric scraps. She hid a few precious, stolen potatoes in the lining.

"With this beautiful outfit," Sabina later remarked tongue-in-cheek, "I came back to Kozienice."

During the brutal trek from the labor camp at Czestochowa in southern Poland to the town of Kozienice one hundred seventy-one miles away, her constant companions were there for support. They had survived the worst of the war by sticking together and caring for one another. Now, as the young women approached the last leg of their miserable journey, they clung to the slimmest glimmer of hope. Perhaps a relative who lived in Kozienice was still alive and waited to welcome them. They longed for the warmth of a wood-fired stove, a bowl of hot soup, a mattress to rest their aching bodies. Mostly, they were anxious for news of their families. "What happened to my father in Warsaw?" Sabina was desperate to ask.

Even as they anticipated freedom, family, and a stomach full of food, they could not escape the all-too-familiar torments. Aching hunger, bitter cold, and the constant fight to stay alive were as much a harsh reality as an excruciating memory that flashed through their minds like lightning bolts and earsplitting thunder in a never-ending storm.

With feet sinking into the deep snow, Sabina and her companions kept northeast to Kozienice. All day, they slogged up hills, down slopes, and across ice-coated waterways, zigzagging around bombed-out roads and bridges past frozen corpses of German soldiers strewn on the roads. As night fell, they knocked on farmhouse doors. Often the structures lay in ruins. Twice, kindly women with tattered headscarves and bony hands let them in. Despite their own lack of necessities, these Polish peasants did not hesitate to scrape some potatoes from a pot or serve them glasses of warm tea. Other unwilling hosts pointed them to abandoned barns. More often, doors closed in their faces.

Finally, Sabina and her companions reached their destination. Even if their longings would be dashed with disappointment, at least they were in a familiar town where the air smelled sweet and scented of pines, where the crystalline river would wash away their sorrows, and where they could live and love and rebuild their lives.

"Then," she sighed, "we met our Poles."

How could it be that hatred toward Jews in Poland was even more malicious after the war than before? The general feeling in the streets was fear, as Sabina described it. "There was a very poor hello, as I would say, on our doors. One day we'll find a note, 'Hey Jew, how did you escape from being a piece of soap?'"

A similar situation confronted them when they thwacked the door of a home formerly owned by a wealthy Jewish family, one of just two or three Jewish structures standing among the rubble and ruins. The house had been taken over by a group of nuns who had no intention of leaving. Standing at the door where the faded outline of a mezuzah greeted them on the doorpost, they could not convince the nuns to let them in. Genya—a feisty lady notwithstanding her tiny stature—stood her ground and argued with them. Still, the holy sisters would not allow them in.

The reappearance of Jewish survivors after the war alarmed the locals. They feared the Jews had come back to reclaim their homes and belongings. After the liquidation of the Kozienice ghetto two-and-a-half years earlier, authorities allowed the Poles to plunder the Jewish homes. Townspeople ransacked the Jews' furniture and property, stole their goods, sold the loot, and took possession of their houses.

Most Poles believed that the Jewish population had been wiped out, never to return. It was not far from the truth. The Germans murdered ninety percent of Poland's Jews—about 3.3 million souls. The fraction that escaped from Hitler's deathly clutches and came back from the camps must have looked to the Poles like vengeful ghosts risen from the grave.

Hit by the awful reality of yet another loss, Sabina choked with emotion. Other than her sister Genya, her entire family was gone—all murdered by the Nazis. The life of her youth was no more. The future looked grim. All her options seemed to end in tears.

But the will to survive did not abandon her. Maybe she thought of her sister, who was still possessed with the spirit to fight for their survival. Or her friend Pola who risked everything in the camps to save her child, little Ruth.

Just then, the nuns gasped in horror. They were alarmed to catch sight of a soldier in Russian uniform pacing the street. The soldier staggered. Was he drunk? A drunken Russian soldier could spell danger. They had heard how Russian soldiers avenged themselves during the war; how they performed cruel sexual acts on any female body, including nuns. This soldier—dirty and stained with blood—looked especially fearsome. Under his arms, he held two broken boards. And he was limping directly toward them.

Genya squinted her eyes to focus on the face of the intruder, who seemed to come out from the woods like an apparition. Deep from the recesses of the past, she found her voice and let out a scream.

"Shmuel?"

Shmuel stopped dead in his tracks in front of the three young women and blinked with faint recognition. One gripped the hand of her seven-year-old daughter. The one peering through spectacles, who had called his name, appeared tiny and frail.

He then caught sight of her younger sister. In his eyes, she looked exceedingly lovely.

The stare from this figure was so unexpected it overwhelmed Sabina with emotion. The man who had emerged filthy, ragged, and maimed seemed to mirror her own brokenness. Feeling so hopelessly lost, homeless, scared, and alone, she romanticized this Jew in a Russian uniform. Could he be a storybook prince destined to find her? Though not a religious woman, she took to heart that Providence had a plan. It was not a stretch to look toward the sky and sigh, Thank God—Gott in Himmel—my help has come!

It took only a few gruff demands from the soldier for the nuns to grab their belongings and make a quick exit out the door. With pounding hearts and trembling bodies, Sabina, Genya, Pola, and little Ruth followed by Shmuel stumbled across the threshold. Their eyes searched the house for some remnant of the well-to-do Jewish family that had resided there. But the room was so grossly transformed to be unrecognizable. Sabina winced. A large wooden cross with the figure of a crucified Jesus covered a spot on the wall that used to display the framed poses of a bearded zaide and head-scarfed bubbe beside the grave stares of their children and grandchildren. Scouring the rooms, not a hint of Judaism remained. The bare wooden kitchen table showed no trace of relatives seated for festive holiday meals or china platters set on an embroidered white tablecloth from mama's dowry. No evidence of Shabbes candlesticks polished to a gleam or eight-branched Chanukah menorah on a curio shelf. No leather-bound Hebrew prayerbooks stacked behind glass-encased shelves. For the homeless survivors, their anticipation of a homecoming felt like a huge letdown. They thought of their own families and household possessions voided and purged as if they had never existed.

Sabina glanced at Shmuel. He stood teary-eyed, transfixed. In time, she would come to expect those tears of sadness whenever he grieved his losses so violently taken by the Nazis. He had sorted the clothing of his relatives while their naked bodies clamored for air in the gas chambers at Treblinka. He had heard their screams. For

177

some inexplicable reason, they all perished, while he stayed alive. Redeemed from slavery, degradation, and death, he remained locked in painful memory of the Holocaust, the faces of loved ones a vision in his dreams.

A throbbing pain from Shmuel's injured leg made him break the silence. "I need to sit," he indicated to the others. Sabina followed his lead and took a seat directly across. It was as if she felt his pain, and her heart went out to him. Ever so gently, they both let down their guard.

Oh, to be a fly on the wall as they confessed, bit by bit, their deep and darkest secrets. They spoke into the tearful and tender night unraveling layers of tragedy until they were bone-weary.

They married on May 14, 1945—not quite one week after Nazi Germany surrendered in defeat. On their wedding day, echoes of crowds cheering and singing against the backdrop of ringing church bells reverberated throughout Europe. Lipstick smudges lingered on the collars of homecoming soldiers. From Times Square to Trafalgar Square, brightly colored streamers and ticker tape still littered the streets.

Such celebrations were a far cry from their own homecomings. No banners, parades, or embraces greeted the unlikely heroes of the Holocaust. Slammed doors took the place of welcome mats. Angry shouts bellowed in their ears.

But in a world reeling from the aftermath of war, Shmuel and Sabina's marriage meant a declaration of optimism and a stake in the future—their healing salve. Between heartthrobs of hopes and dreams, the couple picked up the pieces of their shattered lives and set their sights on the new life they would build together, the family they yearned to create. One day, they would clasp the fingers of their toddler, so pudgy and perfect, and the pitted welts of their own mutilated hands would give urgency to their ambitions. They would mouth promises to their children: Never will you know forced labor and metal splinters from bullets. Never will you know constant fear. Nor the throbbing pangs of hunger. You will never smell the sickening stench of human slaughter. You will never have to fight for your life just to exist one more day.

Shmuel and Sabina wiped their tears. They had endured the deepest depths of agony and outlived the darkest years of history. From the seeds of remembrance, they would plant the legacy of a family so that the children of their children might one day return and hear the sweet refrain: "Welcome home."

Poetry

Introduction

Connecticut is home. It is where we return after finding stories in other people's neighborhoods and countryside. It is where we build our nests. Whether homegrown or transplanted—to be planted. We burrow amongst the maple trees and lilac clusters to write poetry or prose. Some may reminisce about the tobacco fields where you dared to spend summers growing browner than the leaves you picked to dry. My family roots stretch like those rows of fields, from the troubling history of Malaga Island, Maine to the sharecroppers of South Carolina, my grandparents made Bloomfield, Connecticut, their homestead since 1954. Even though I was born in Connecticut and raised here most of my life, I grew up experiencing many different parts of the world, especially during my early poetic life as a co-slam master for the Hartford Slam Team competing at the National Slam Competitions. Traveling elsewhere helped me come back home and see Connecticut's wonders.

This selection of poems is much like the New England foliage. Some poems recount experiences right in their "Neighborhood," while others reach beyond the "Occupied Territories" of the world. I was drawn to the quintessential imagery of leaves crunching underfoot and the cold Mystic shoreline, mixed with the human landscape of "Addicts on a Park Bench" in New Haven. The profound tension found in the speakers of these poems, whose experiences may have happened elsewhere in the world, yet the creator, a poet nestled in our state's borders, is a testament to the importance of the journey we take as travelers—moving in thought from places of great sorrow to the joy we find in the most minor observations of this fantastic planet.

The poems' ordering fell in place, much like the autumn leaves that gather around the oldest church. Each poem spoke to a season;

one of Connecticut's most beautiful aspects due to its location in the Northeast. I am blessed to have had the opportunity to read so many thought-provoking poems. I applaud all the poets who painted the page with their hearts and thoughts. I want to thank the editorial team and interns for assembling a mosaic display of literature. And I hope you, the reader, enjoy the journey these poems take you on beyond the Connecticut landscape to see and feel our world in ways we can only conjure with our words.

Summer Tate

Return to My Neighborhood

By Nancy Manning

Windsor Locks sleeps. But I remember livelier times.
Mike the milkman walking up our sidewalk as bottles clinked. He
tipped his hat, deposited our order in the metal bin, took the empties.

In front of Cobbs' house, the soda man parked his rusty van that
often backfired. Though I never saw him or what he delivered, I
always asked my mother why couldn't we drink soda?

The delivery man in sooty overalls dumped a load of coal outside
Gertie's cellar. Into her eighties, she'd shovel the black rocks into
a bin for her furnace. I'd hear the scrape of metal on cement.

Boys filled our backyard for a game of baseball. Batters
aimed for left field, strained to hit a ball at our cow barn,
shatter an unlucky window for us cheering fans.

We cluttered our den on hot summer afternoons to watch *Dark
Shadows*. My brother repositioned rabbit ears to adjust our
failing TV. Without a fan, all us kids sweated, didn't mind.

In our clubhouse, we reenacted vampire and werewolf scenes.
Screamed when we were attacked. We hosted loud Halloween parties,
awarded prizes for the best costume, fastest bob for apple.

In winter we ice skated on Babiarz's pond. Blades glided as we
tried to figure skate graceful spins like Peggy Fleming. Boys

tore up the ice as they slammed a puck into a net of twigs.

We formed a kids' club. Held meetings by the chicken coop,
chanted a theme song—*Blackberry Hills, rah, rah, rah.*
Surrendered thumbs for pin pricks and blood promises.

We skipped to hopscotch in the driveway, shouted to Bob the Polish
man who walked by, returned home with a brown paper bag under
one arm. We rode bikes on a driveway course marked

by sheetrock chalk. Oftentimes, I raced up Sunset Street,
flew back down, my arms extended out like I was flying,
like I would be a kid forever.

Hartford Living

By Tiffany Washington

Midday I cross Capan at Garden
to Johnson's for catfish.
How can I ever love anything in this world?
Beneath the blinking light, above rusted rim,
the pot-holed road, a T.V. on the curb,
girls are still jumping rope.

August in the Northeast Kingdom

By Elisabeth Kennedy

I.

Some mornings, if I'm lucky,
I catch that fleeting light
shimmering across
the rippled lake
as it grazes
the pitched roof
of the timeworn cabin.

I catch the glimmer,
the flash,
the verdant beauty
& I sit with breath slow,
hands loose,
& my heart syncs
with the lake & forest.

II.

Robins, the earliest birds,
sing their secrets. I know,
without knowing,
without words,
what it means.

III.

At dawn, amidst dreams
of wood fairies & campfires,
I memorize the character
of the worn floorboards,
padding bare feet stealthily
over cool wood, padding early
without a creak, soundless
as the morning owl arcing
onto the forest floor,
undetectable on taut wings.

& thus, with my body,
I have swiftly learned truths
of this Eden, a refuge surely loved
many summers by many hearts
filled full of all the mornings of mists
wisping up traces of life
rising out of the warmth
of conical spires
ringing the cool water.

IV.

Mid-horizon, still
morning, dark shapes
of loons floating
announce the day,
calling mournfully
to other loons, to anyone
who might listen.

If the Universe Can Grow and Expand, Why Shouldn't I?

By Natalie Schriefer

I leave you
at the train station,
doors
swooshing
shut between us.

We've been fraying
for weeks,
like the hem
of a shirt—each
wash unfurling
another inch
of seam.
I have only
made it
official.

When galaxies grow
apart, it's called
recessional
velocity—
but we're no
stars, just
empty space,
the space

between you
on the platform

and me
on the train
elongating
like light
stretched
across an
event horizon—
there's no
going back.
You don't want
to change,
and I can't stay
the same,
not anymore.

Moving the Goal Post

By Chelsea Dodds

Three weeks after graduation,
we meet in the high school parking lot
to go skateboarding.

The humid afternoon breeze
tickles my legs below my Bermuda
shorts. I've not yet learned to love my
thighs.

While you tighten my trucks,
I ride your bike too fast around the tennis court
and fall into the fence.

The bruise will make a good story
later. Something tangible beyond
late-night AIM chats, our friendship
blossoming

behind computer screens, out of sight from
the rest of the world. I want to believe
something magical is rising with the stars

visible from the football field,
where we go to cool off and talk.
I sit cross-legged in the grass

and you hang upside down
on the goal post, despite my
protests. I think we'd be cute
together.

But you dream of living in New York City
and I dream of living in the woods,
in a town smaller than this one,

so I try to not let you see
me swallow my disappointment
at what can never be.

I Keep Writing Epitaphs

By Jen Payne

Last night, I snuck
across the pond
to the half-cut trees,
their slaughtered limbs
strewn across the yard
of the large new house,
and listened while
spiders and ants
and all small things
evacuated, slowly.
I knelt below the
one last Maple
in whose branches
I once spied
turkeys sleeping
and apologized
in whispers
that sounded like
midnight bird wings,
while my tears
collected in pools
around her sweet trunk
and we listened
as the stars departed
and the sun rose
and the marsh hawk
came to pay its
last respects.

A Cento for Covid's Garden

By Heidi St. Jean

A walk through the garden
sets off the mind's tripwires —
it coaxes me to the vapor and dust.
One hour loosens from the sockets
of another.
It has been a hard season for bodies,
for the given strangeness of care.
Bury the broken thinking
in the backyard with the herbs.
I can do nothing.
I stand here as if lost.
You with your smoke-eyes are all-seeing,
predaceous and singular —
de-root me from this garden.
Why leave a dead thing dangling?
Short of breath, my grief as large
as a daughter's. Alone in such an hour
my body is a scar, aching:
I have not spoken to my mother in years.
I have taken the shape of her hips.
The rain's not yet done, but the light
comes feeling its way back, as it does.
La Luna renews itself,
and you can too.
A single twist of the stem
and summer falls into my hands.
I travel from June to June, seeking —

I too would romp
in that wild phosphorescence,
to live always in the possible...
I just came to this life again,
alive in my silent way.
Last night I dreamed
I could only save one person;
there's a man I love —
we are sap and vine and solstice.
Plunge us into sleep and deliquescence.
If the vine grows freely,
it will scale the vault of the stars.
We are made of dreams and bones.

"A Cento for COVID's Garden" is an original work comprised entirely of lines from poets' works published in the collection "Leaning Toward Light: Poems for Gardens and the Hands That Tend Them," edited by Tess Taylor, (c) 2023, published by Storey Publishing. The poets, in order of appearance: Jenny Xie, Walt Whitman, Jenny Xie, Jason Myers, Ada Limón, Thom Gunn, Brynn Saito, Mary Jo Salter, David Biespiel, Ruben Quesada, Jenny Xie, Mariane Goycoechea, Jacqueline Kolosov, Brynn Saito, Tess Taylor, Jason Myers, Ada Limón, Kiran Kapur, Ann Fisher-Wirth, David Mallet. The word "daughter's" replaces "son's" from D. Biespiel's original line.

Fall Ritual

By Joan Riordan

One day
once a year
every October
the kitchen is filled with
     crinkling plastic wrappers
     beeps and dings of the microwave
     the thick, sweet smell of melted caramel
     coating waxy-red apples –
          with sticks we gouged into the tops
     set to cool on milky wax paper.

In time
darkness blackens windows
one lamp warms the living room.
It's my year.
     I press play and –
     We're off to see the Wizard!

Clutching caramel apples,
     blankets,
       stuffed animals
we squeeze onto the couch –
together
anticipating with dread
and eagerness
the arrival
of winged monkeys.

Blueberry Pie For Breakfast

By Jess Rawling

Whippoorwill wakes me like a prophecy,
woody lilt from August leaves
already turning to compost. Ruby dawn,
thunderheads, blueberry pie in the oven,
coffee. Lord, the coffee.

The ocean hushes us from behind a dune
at the end of the pond;
or is it an edge we walk along,
while the sea bites at the sand wall?

    I didn't swim this summer,
    but I swear my feet left the ground
    when I waded in that one time —
    Jonah says it doesn't count unless my head
    goes under   whip-poor-will
                    whip-poor-will
                           whip-poor-will

Lord, the coffee. Smoky steam
pairing itself with the storm's
lightning sizzle, our socked feet
brushing the bricked kitchen floor,
herbaceous, spiced and buttery taste
of blueberry pie staining our teeth
purple.

I feel godless, like a night bird
loam-lurking, swallowing
crickets whole while their singing rages on
like a barn rave.

Addicts On a Park Bench Near Old Campus, New Haven

By David Capps

Like two turtledoves mated for life, who watch fall leaves
slide down onto wet cement the color of their own feathers
caked, cracked, sectioned into blocks, defecated upon daily,

as twigs from their nest settle like spring ash, spring's meth-
mouth prompts them to drop sweet caress below their loft's
rude décollage of trash, that one grey egg might break open

the self-proclaimed fortress of Yale, so they kiss each other.

Thanksgiving, New Haven

By David Capps

The golden glowing interiors of houses filled with the laughter
of children.
The boisterousness of living rooms.

Gutters emptied of slimy ace bandages, leaf-stuffed abysses, needles,
crack pipes.

Lincoln street smells like gravy though it is windless where I have
been walking
pondering the solitude of the mean.

Old Saxophone

By Jack Sheedy

It's yours now, Joel. I hope you can restore it,
this skinny letter S of tarnished brass
that hasn't blown a note in thirty years.

When Dad died, no one else could make it sing.
And now look at it: scratched and dull and
dimpled from reedless mouthpiece down to muted
bell.

It's an alto, says the music shop repairman,
and pitched below what's normal—it won't play
along with instruments correctly tuned.

Isn't that just like my dad, your
grandfather? The music that he played,
no one could join, an almost minor key, not
quite resolved

like his imperfect life beyond his music.
He let me blow it once: a mallard's squawk!
He chuckled at my lousy embouchure.

I blamed it on a loosened ligature,
or cracked and dried-up reed—but then he
blew a long and perfect, mournful middle D,

and I admitted that the fault was mine!
I lack the breath, I lack the stamina,
I lack the carefree passion that he had,

that made up for his lack of fine technique,
unpolished, like this twisted instrument.
I ask one thing, Joel, when you get it fixed:

come visit and play "My Old Man" for me.
Then let me try my embouchure again.
Teach me to pucker, teach me how to kiss,

to cushion lower lip to moistened reed,
and take a breath, and blow a perfect note
from this same alto sax my daddy played.

Like Smoke

By Ginny Lowe Connors

A large fish jumps, transcending, momentarily
its boundary of water. Across the inlet
something crackles, licking at twilight—
bonfire on the shore. The dance of its orange
flames in black water a flare of surprise,
bright reflection on a dark canvas.

Fire on water, simple fact, brilliant dream. A plume of
smoke billows up behind the trees, loses itself in the
breath of an autumn night. Half clouded over, the
moon is rising too, not quite full. Every existence a
process of becoming.

It's when I let go of myself, dissolve
into the fabric, that I become most myself,
become night air pressing at window glass,
become the moth with its dusty wings.

Flame leaping across water, moon
with its cloak of cloud, those are what I
am, and I am the fish, too, briefly flying.

St. Thomas Preparatory Seminary, 1956

By Bill Conlon

I read of eighty-one-year-old Arthur Perrault's sentence
to thirty years in prison for sexual abuse of one boy out
of as many as eighty whom he harmed.
Three of his young victims committed suicide
before they reached the age of eighteen. I remember
my freshman year at the six-year prep school.

Breezes whisked through, cooled a copse of pines
on a late September afternoon, and teased
the pages of *Ivanhoe*. Needles, fallen from above,
provide a mattress. The scent of pine cones
took me to medieval England with Scott's
enchanting tale of knights and knaves.

Footsteps crunching on nature's carpet preceded
Arthur's presence, blocking the light
filtered through the trees. The college man sat,
cross-legged and uninvited. He complemented
a shot I made on the basketball court and started
questioning my thoughts and habits of sex.

This behavior discomfited me. My confessor best coped with
carnal questions. Arthur's lower lip, folded out and down,
revealed its moist pink interior, repulsing me. I sat, caught
between enduring this intrusion and insulting a man four years
my senior. I claimed time pressure for my reading, asked
Arthur to let me return to Sherwood Forest.

Sixty-some years later, captured Arthur comes
cuffed from Tangier to face charges of harming
children.
I wonder how many of my classmates he hurt,
        how many in the classes after mine in the years that he
remained at St. Thomas. Should I have reported misgivings?
        Would anyone have listened to an overly scrupulous boy, or
                                did they know and look away,
                                        ordain
                                        a monster?

Tangible

By Elizabeth Alfonzo

I like to hear leaves crunch and rake
on the pavement behind me
because then I know
wind is real
I feel it pushing against my body
in the afternoon sun of winter
and my body against it
then I know I am real
as real as the sound
of leaves rustling

Something Ragged

By Dana J. Graef

In the early days when sunlight
came only at an angle, through dusty
windows that I hadn't cleaned, I
grew intent on mending. I gathered
old wool and ripped up flannel,
torn towels and threadbare
jeans. When I woke, our world
was unraveling; it was pulling apart
at the seams. At night I chose to work
with soft and shining things: gold
scissors that cut like the beak
of a heron, silver needles that fell
to the floor, marled grey wool and
blue cotton thread. For all those ragged
edges. But even as I mended, life
still split

        and frayed. I saw it more
and more, this perpetual undoing. It
came in the morning and left with
the light. Forgiveness—when I find you—
I will bury my knots in your seams.

Again

By Robert Cording

I am walking again, the same paths
walked day-after-day six years
ago when my son died. There are
the few houses in the distance,
the dark pond in the foreground,
the little bridge over the marsh
still to come but always before me. I
knelt there once, or collapsed, the
guardrail my makeshift altar. In the
earliest morning after my son died, I
said, *Daniel, my child.* What kind of
foolish arrogance expected
a chipping sparrow to answer, *father.*
And now, here I am still trying
to outwalk my mind's thoughts.

The sun burnishes the tops of trees,
warms the cold winter fields.
When I enter the woods' maze
of branches, it's as if I am
disappearing; underfoot, blanched
leaves
already lacey with decomposition.
The silence here seeps into me
as if I was porous. I am waiting for
something in me to change, to
respond to the deepening gold-blue
bars of light that slip between
the trees with something like delight's
unexpected appearance, and glints in
the understory of deer-pathed
rhododendron and mountain laurel.

Bombogenesis

By Elisabeth Kennedy

I.
We did not know your name
as the snow fell fat & heavy,
melting, as it touched the warm road.
The snow began to stick & we wondered,
as we always do, whether tomorrow
would be a snow day.

Our family put on puffy coats & thick-soled boots
for a walk in the crisp snow-dusted streets,
footprints tracing haphazard delight
in the freshening, as we always do.

Returning home, sun warming the still bright rooms,
we drank hot milk with honey, a sweetness
in the insistent falling & we collected orphan socks
for sewing projects we knew would keep us entertained
during tomorrow's no-school-pajamas-only kind of day,
as the snow continued falling for the plows to clear
with their terrible scraping & growling, as they always do.

II.

As night fell, you sped over warmed ocean waters, gaining momentum,
moving into a dreadful churning, cyclone winds insistently circling
your cold empty heart, you, a mad swirling comma chasing its tail
& we watched from our warm rooms the snow flying in terrible
gusts, one hundred & two miles per hour, bending the bones of trees,
crying & wailing in its fury, wind & snow that blew & raged
& plows that circled & strained up the hills with a groaning,
urged on by drivers who could no longer see the road, an endless sea
of white on white, everything white, & all the drivers wanted
was to clear the roads, & go home.

Hour after hour the plows & their drivers pressed on in the street-lit night, & we put the
children to bed & peeked out at the no-longer-familiar street, a whiteout of drifting snow &
we watched from our warm windows as the night became frozen & strange, as the drifts
pressed up the stop sign poles & white snow touched the red octagons & we listened to the
howl of the storm & wondered if we would be trapped in snow like never before & we
worried & hoped we would not lose power & grow cold like this startling night & the plow
lights shone a beastly yellow as they struggled around the corners & the snow got deeper &
deeper, & we
sleepless & deep into nightfall saw the last plow make its final tired pass up the
hill & grind to a screeching halt
                              on Morris Street,   & the world was
enveloped
in the silence & the blowing
          of a great & terrible snow.

III.

The next day, the sun rose quietly over the horizon of snow-iced trees
& glanced blindingly off the frozen world. Snow had drifted up
past the window sills & the doors of all the houses were sealed shut.

House after house, street after street, cocooned in snow. Houses pushing up gallantly out of the
thick glacier of snow, the ice-flow, that had erased what we knew of our navigable world.

In the brightened rooms, only house sounds remained, the chug & hiss of the coffeemaker, the
soft hum of the fridge, the breaths of the sleeping children, & the occasional damp thuds of rafts
of snow sliding from the pitched roof onto more snow. Snow upon snow upon snow.

Outside was oddly quiet. The storm's greatness had rendered all the snowblowers useless,
hushing whole towns for miles & miles — & the world was brand new again. It was cold, so
very cold, & the snow had settled in, as the house had settled in, & we had settled in. We
remember silence as the only thing we could hear & we wondered who might reach us first.

We were lucky. We never lost power, so the children drank peppermint tea & ate buttered toast & set
to long days of sewing projects, blanket forts, puzzling, & invented games. They wanted to
slide out the window & disappear into the snow like the fathers did. Those fathers who wanted to find
a way out (to where I don't know) or like our family, who had to dig out to the chickens to
bring them warm water & food.

I remember the simplicity of the determined shoveling. Man vs. snow, a human machine in royal blue
snow pants, the only color in a whitened world. The swishing of the fabric & the
grunt/scoop/thunk of the act of shoveling. Snow being launched into air from blue into blue,
lifting & falling, softly, rhythmically, white on white, snow upon snow.

For longer than it took for the world to be created, the Army Corps of Engineers, starting at the shore,
dumped truckloads of snow & ice into Long Island Sound. The radio told us they were
working through the night in shifts & it took seven whole days before they were able to reach us
in the epicenter. We heard their engines approaching days before we saw the cumbersome
camouflaged vehicles at the end of our street, ridiculous & welcome, rolling against the perfect

snow & everything beneath it, yard ornaments, fences, hedges.

We began to worry about the plow drivers. We hoped they were home, wearing warm socks, baking bread & stitching striped rabbits with blue ears out of all the orphans they could find, & as we looked back, one by one the neighbors snowblowers emerged, filling up the streets with an industrious throbbing and rumbling, claiming the peace of the clean world.

The Student Cooks Dinner During Class

By Pat Mottola

I think I'm hallucinating.
Maybe my TV is on and I'm
watching *Giada at Home*
or *Barefoot Contessa* or
Rachael Ray. I blink.

I teach online,
Zoom University.
Allie is in her kitchen
stirring about at 5 p.m.,
quite cozy in her square
on my computer screen.

I ask what she is doing
and she says, *cooking*.
Yes, this one tiny moving square
a cartoon cel come to life
in this mosaic of faces. I imagine
what she is cooking. Sounds
of onions being chopped,
fish frying, blender blending.
Finally the fork against the plate.

Suddenly I'm hungry. I excuse myself
and go fix a sandwich. A grilled cheese.
Am I allowed to do that?
I think back to my own college years. Crabby
Miss Varmette, my sociology professor. No one
even chewed gum in class.
Pay attention or else.

Back to the present. No one missed me.
Allie's square is now dark.
Students are texting. Maybe DoorDash?
I am content, even grateful.
For the inspiration.
The break.
The food for thought.

Fugue for What Passes

By Ginny Lowe Connors

snowflakes	on his lashes		moments	only memory can	hold
like so many	stars		in the wilderness, our lives	flicker, flare	and spark
silent	tears		bloom briefly	like fireflies	before love disappears
petals	tremble and fall		fade away	in the garden	unnoticed
brief beauty	unsolvable		as dreams	I want you back	let the song continue

The Placid Dervish

By Ed Ahern

Whirling naked in a crowded room,
before those hated and loved,
beside things once lusted for,
become what I do not understand,
but am at last at peace with.
The peeling of my posturings
has laid bare a gnarly being
content in his deformities,
which is as close to happy
as I would care to be.

The Holy Land /
The Occupied Territories

By Katherine E. Schneider

Driving back to Bethlehem on a clear, winter night—
my memory of it now makes it wider.

I return from a village perched on a hillside
carved with ancient terraces like each hill in the vista

seating homes, holding orchards, each catching sunshine:
all living, breathing testaments to the people of Palestine.

Now between the last evening and first morning prayer,
I almost forgot occupation was there, that man-made

oppression's hideous gears were churning under distant
stars of the sky among the silent, narrow roads and minaret lights.

I watched the twists and turns—ascending, descending.
So many stone buildings with people dreaming inside.

I almost forgot at that time—that tucked into the shadows of the land
were the cold cenotaphs and apathetic bones of patriarchs in their hallowed crypts,

bare to air ruins of emperors and kings, the lingering echoes of prophets' warnings.
Somewhere crushed to powder was the broken jar of perfume—

the landing-place of Jesus' tears, the execution site,
the empty tomb.

City On A Hill

By Katherine E. Schneider

You are the light of the world.
A city on a hill cannot be hidden. -Matthew 5:14

I am a city on a hill—
I know what Jesus meant,
I saw it myself—

I saw the cities on the hills in the Holy Land.

Out of the terminal, into the van,
we drove through the night
Israeli street to Palestine.

I saw the cities on the hills—

they sparkled in the black ore
of the crisp January sky
exposed, twinkling, bright.

I am a city on a hill, eyes fixed to the window,

and when we crossed
the army-guarded checkpoint
into the town

the scene came more to life—

Christmas decorations
strung up across the streets
parallel parking, car beeps.

I swear I saw a man riding a horse inexplicably.

The driver made friends with me—
he stopped to buy *kunafa;*
we ate it as he drove

with sticky fingers.

And there I was in a hotel in Bethlehem,
moved from a basic room
to one with a balcony—

I could see out from inside the city.
Each day I looked out,
I walked around
the ancient places and the newly-built

I thought about what it means to be a city and a light.

And what are all the structures and things
except dust not yet pounded out?

And what really matters except
the lives of the people who live now?

And if this was the longitude and latitude
where Christ was born and is no more—

then ours are the mortal bodies that hold the holy wisdom
and the option to conjure life with its power.

People are the only holy cities,
the contrast in the silent night—

we are the living truth cast on the screen of time—

Why I Write Poems: An Ars Poetica

By B. Fulton Jennes

When older sisters were dispatched to school
and slate-dull hours yawned before us,
when she'd tossed seed to the birds and pulled sheets
tight on every bed, when washed plates were
clatter-stowed in high cupboards and laundry tangoed
in the enamel tub, when the steam iron ceased its hiss
over starched white shirts and crisp school skirts, when
I had sat on my hands in that silent seat, watching and
waiting, waiting and watching, no word exchanged
between us, no touch, no gaze—she'd sink-sigh onto
her hard chair, drag a ragged sleeve across the
morning's sweat, tap a sleek white cylinder from the
red pack waiting on the table, put it to her lips,
strike a stuttering match, and breathe.

I knew not to interrupt those moments of ease.
But when her eyes at last lifted from linoleum
and recognized the waiting world, I'd venture
Mama, I wrote you a poem, remembering her joy,
sudden and seldom, when a sister's poem
was printed in the mimeographed PTA newsletter
sent home in a bookbag that smelled of ink and envy.

And she'd say *Bring it here then. Let's have a look.*
I'd hand her the scrap of paper covered, every inch,
with electric scribbles, preliterate lightning,
desperate to speak, to mean. Then
I'd sit on her lap and say *You read it, Mama.*
And she would.

Out in the snow

By Tim Stobierski

a rabbit hops
from beneath
the dormant forsythia,
zigzags across
the front yard's slope,
plants itself
on the left side
of the old mailbox,
still angled
from that night
— (which night?) —
eons ago
when dad had too much wine,
backed into it with his truck,
and gave the earth its tilt.

Here, again.
Even this poem,
which began about a rabbit
in the snow,
finds its way to you —
the rabbit, gone;
the snow, gone;
and you.

The Singer Machine

By Jeff Schwartz

Diane sends me the photo
of our grandmother's sewing machine
crouched in a corner, polished black with
gold Singer script & silver throat plate,
circa 1933. She's cleaning the house for a
stager in Cleveland who won't
let anything stay as it is. The dining room
(formerly Peach) has to be painted Smoke Tan.
The 60s record cabinet has to be pitched.
Diane's gorgeous oak desk must go. What a mess!
And those plants—
twenty years of intimate care—
they block the window. Clutter's
the enemy for prospective buyers
who will want to imagine
their own stuff in an empty
house. But not too empty or
it'll feel abandoned. And there
are already too many of those
in Cleveland. The question is
where to hide the sewing machine
& those boxes of family papers, stained
with the smoke of personal history.
Our grandmother ran into a fire
to save that machine. It was the only thing she
couldn't let go.

Ozymandias: My Father Dug a Pond

By B. Fulton Jennes

When a walk to the brook led him past a spring
erupting one April thaw, my father saw a pond
stocked with trout for fishing, iced in winter

to keep children outside, away, skating, a cheapskate
alternative to trips to Crystal Lake in summer, where
kids paid 50 cents—*highway robbery!*—to swim.

So he called Tom Cipperley, hired him to excavate
with his big digger for a hundred bucks a day. The
new pond filled quickly: 50 feet wide, three times

as long, six feet deep in the middle, with a clay bottom
and water so clean you could drink while you swam.
My mother fished for eels and fried them. We learned

to skate backwards, face off against boys on center ice.
Once, I emerged with a leech fixed to my belly, but
even that insult didn't keep us away. For a decade,

the pond delighted us all. But then Dad's hunting dog
was shot by a neighboring farmer. The barn collapsed
on his '47 Ford, nearly rebuilt. His youngest daughter

smoked pot, ran with the wrong crowd, skipped school.
And the banks of the pond were undermined by muskrats.
Rains carried backhoed dirt back to its source. Willows fell,

lifting their tortured roots to the sky. The pond grew smaller
every year. Now nothing beside remains but a marsh-bound
spring that burbles in April, sounding so much like laughter.

Black Grapevine

inspired by the novel, Roots

By Frederick-Douglass Knowles II

the *black grapevine*
unravels the massacre
unclenches the scent
of Tulsa's barren arms
hooded ghosts roasting
colored children in a
town of eternal flame
their infant ash sailing
along the breath of the
Mississippi my second
great-grandfather *Peg*
-Leg Dan sleeps one
-limb up in the corner
of their Ocala home
my great-grandmother
Donie Fullwood blackens
the bottom of cornbread
while counting her bullets
my grandmother Martha
finishing fourth grade dreams
of sunny-blue babies bouncing
in a lap of blaze stale shadows
waft the horizon of their home
Peg-Leg levels his rifle out the window
Fullwood steals cross

yard brands the barrel
of her Colt into the nape
of the hooded ghost
dousing supremacy on
the fur of their front lawn
a thumb-steady click an
ignition of blackness a
swamp of blood a parish
of fiendish men scuttle
like frightened children
spooked by ghosts a
vigilant fourth grader
silent-eyed in the attic
witnesses her mother
denature a flea plucked
from the pelt of her
freedom the *black*
grapevine unravels
an uprising in Ocala
the midnight stance
of a rifled one-legged
man a lucid fourth grader
and a corn bread blackening
Cherokee trigger
thumb-steady
Great-grandmother

Commence

By Steven Ostrowski

Moving on for my mother
came late spring
in the tunnel-deep, machine-blink night
of the oncology ward.

In her final room, 4 a.m., morphing
toward paradise on a morphine drip,
I asked her if she was ready.

She dribbled a little bile
into the sliver cup I held
steady as I could
under her chin.

When time slowed
to almost stop,
I gazed so closely at her face
that I witnessed her
simplified to essence,
a single point of stillness;
a great beauty
exposed by mystery.

As ever, her eyes
in awe of everything.

Tubular light, heart graph
barely moving, blip by blip,
I felt an intimacy
I'd never known
with such certainty.

I stroked her damp hair
and kissed her high cheekbone.
I paced a little,
to unweaken my legs.
She beckoned me back.
With my ear to her mouth,
her breath like Easter flowers,
she couraged, "Yes. I am."

Fight No. 3

By Mary Vallo

My breath releases in hard huffs we both can hear
while my arms can't decide where to place themselves
till a fist forms in the hand under the pillow
and my head turns away so my eyes don't stare
and that's how I know you will read these signals
which right about now are as big as a billboard
in neon with marching band and special effects
that will make you lean over, touching
with a tentative hand to ask
what's wrong and I will say nothing
which of course not only means something
but the something we've said so many times before
that I am really really really trying to stay so still
that it doesn't come out because if it does
(cue the tears, push the hand away)
it will start somewhere in the middle and I think
that it's best for all concerned if it doesn't
so maybe we could just give this a name
or a number, say No. 3, and you can check
the legend on your map of me
and find where it is we are without
actually going there
and I can simply close my eyes
and finally finally finally go
to sleep.

Finding Exile

By Jen Payne

Preparing herself for the inevitable,
the sandpiper —
usually found along the coast
makes her home now
by a small pond in the woods
three miles from the Sound.
It's quiet here, most days,
except when the wind
carries clamor from the south,
and she's been welcomed
graciously
by the turtles and frogs,
the heron and wood ducks.
They've come here, too,
this protected space
with ample shade and shallows
to share with anyone who needs
asylum from the rising conflict.
You might say we are refugees,
displaced from the familiar
by forces not of our making
finding exile here,
making life despite the storm,
saying grace for the bounty.

Bridgeportmanteau
By Adrian Dallas Frandle

Each mouth a five star motel for new creations.
New havens for language, nurtured in the lush

valleys of adventurous tongues. Listen,
a seraphriend came down to announce

that compound words are the shortest poems
one can make, like delicate pairs of lace socks

packed snug in a child's portmanteau
suitcase. Wordkissing terms bear new

creatures into life from pieces of sound,
creating whole new definitions. Like lovers

who conjoin over Zoom across borderlines &
timezones, words are transfixed by the presence

of each others' likeness, despite distance.
Whether consplosion of compassion or a handclasp

through rubble, we are as togetherbound by speech
as sky to lark, as plug to spark, as rhyme to sound.

O gathering place on the page, O membrane of meaning,
your process of soft osmosis we undertake on the road

from head-to-heartspace. You make every crossroad
crossable, every hedgeline an invitation to open field:

    say not stranger
    when you mean *godkin* or *starmate*
    say *angelips* not beloved &
    instead of thank you
    say *blessfate.*

Contributors

Ed Ahern
Ed Ahern resumed writing after forty-odd years in foreign intelligence and international sales. He's had over 450 stories and poems published so far, and ten books. Ed works the other side of writing at *Bewildering Stories* where he manages a posse of eight review editors, and as lead editor at *Scribes Microfiction*.

Sharbari Ahmed
Sharbari is a novelist, screenwriter, and professor. She lives in Darien with two rescue dogs and a son nearby.

Elizabeth Alfonzo
Elizabeth Alfonzo is a poet and physical therapist living outside of New Haven, CT. Her writing has been published in *Please See Me*, *Caesura, Snapdragon: A Journal of Art & Healing, Here, and Waking Up to the Earth Anthology* with Grayson Books. Her empathy and deep connection to her ancestors guides her writing.

Liz Bullard
Liz Bullard is a passionate author, podcast host, coach, and self-published writer. She's currently signed to Tabletop Publishing and eagerly awaits the publication of her first children's book. Liz loves reading and storytelling and has immersed herself in the world of writing. As a coach she helps writers find clarity, overcome creativity limiting beliefs, and develop effective organizational skills to achieve their goals. When she's not working, Liz enjoys cooking with her corgi Preston by her side and curling up with a good book.

David Capps

David Capps is a philosophy professor and poet who lives in New Haven, CT. He is the author of four chapbooks: *Poems from the First Voyage* (The Nasiona Press, 2019), *A Non-Grecian Non-Urn* (Yavanika Press, 2019), *Colossi* (Kelsay Books, 2020), and *Wheatfield with a Reaper* (Akinoga Press, forthcoming). His latest work, *On the Great Duration of Life*, a riff on Seneca's *On the Shortness of Life*, is available from Schism Neuronics.

Michael Todd Cohen

Michael Todd Cohen's work appears in *The Rumpus*, *Split/Lip*, *Columbia Journal*, and *Pithead Chapel*, among others, and has been included in *Best Micro Fictions*, *The Connecticut Literary Anthology*, and nominated for a Pushcart Prize. He lives with a poet-husband and two illiterate chihuahuas, by a rusty lighthouse, in New England. For more: michaeltoddcohen.com.

Bill Conlon

Bill Conlon received his MFA in Creative Writing at Southern Connecticut State University in May 2023. He previously earned his B.A. degree in liberal studies at SCSU. He retired from the active work force after an eclectic entrepreneurial career. His chapbook, *Speaking of the Sixties in Verse*, was published in April 2021 by Flying Horse Press. Bill lives with his wife, Debbi, near the beach in West Haven, CT, where he ponders the wonders of life while watching the tides ebb and flow.

Robert Cording

Robert Cording has published ten books of poetry, the latest of which is *In the Unwalled City* (Slant, 2022). His work has appeared in *Hudson Review*, *Southern Review*, *Poetry*, *The Sun*, *New Ohio Review*, *Georgia Review*, *Shenandoah*, *Image*, *32 Poems*, and many other magazines. His work has appeared in two Pushcart Anthologies, in Best American Poetry, and Best Spiritual Poetry. He has been awarded two NEA fellowships in Poetry and two Connecticut Arts Fellowships in Poetry.

Chelsea Dodds

Chelsea Dodds is a high school English teacher and lifelong Connecticut resident. She earned her MFA in fiction from Southern Connecticut State University and concentrated in creative writing as an undergrad at UConn. Her poems and stories have been published in *Rejection Letters, Maudlin House, Poetry Super Highway*, and *Sixfold Journal*. When Chelsea is not writing or teaching, you can usually find her hiking, practicing yoga, or planning her next big road trip. You can read more of her work at chelseadodds.com.

Adrian Dallas Frandle

Adrian Dallas Frandle (they/he) is a Connecticut-based poet and queer fish who writes to the world about its future. They are Poetry Acquisitions Editor for *Variant Press. Book of Extraction: Poems with Teeth* is out now with Kith Books. Read more at adriandallas.com

Jessica Galán

Jessica Galán teaches social studies and English in Hartford, CT. She has been awarded fellowships through the Highlights Foundation and Kweli. Her fiction has been published in *Kweli* and *Huizache Magazine*.

Laura Garrity

Laura Garrity is a writer from Derby, Connecticut. She is a member of the Fairfield County Writers Group and The Written Word at the MAC. She has previously had stories published in the anthologies

Call of the Wyld and *We Who Are About to Die*, and in audio format on the Overcast podcast.

Beth Gibbs

Beth Gibbs, M.A. is an award-winning writer of fiction and non-fiction for mainstream audiences. Her work has appeared in *The Connecticut Literary Anthology* (2020 and 2021), *These Black Bodies Are---A Blacklandia Anthology* (June 2023) and *The Journey Writers Literary Anthology* (2023). She is the author of three books: *Enlighten Up! Finding Clarity, Contentment and Resilience in a Complicated World*; *Soul Food: Life-Affirming Stories Served with Side dishes and Just Desserts*; and *Ogi Bogi The Elephant Yogi: Stories About Yoga for Children*. Her personal blog can be found at: https://www.bethgibbs.com/enlightenup

Kristina Giliberto

Kristina is a writer of essays and stories for all ages. She is a Restorative Yoga teacher and certified in equine therapy. A former reporter, Kristina lives in Connecticut where she enjoys spending time with her husband, three children, and two spoiled dogs.

Sharon Citrin Goldstein

Sharon Citrin Goldstein has expressed her creative passions through multiple careers as an educator, business entrepreneur, and ordained Cantor. For nearly two decades, she directed the Anti-Defamation League's antisemitism programs in Connecticut empowering students and adults to confront the world's longest hatred. Her stories on family and ancestry have been published by *Moment Magazine*, *Jewishgen.org*, *Exploring Judaism*, *Ancestor Strong*, *Sacred Sounds of the Cantors Assembly*, and *Tell Your Story Challenge of West Palm Beach* where she was a short-story finalist. She is currently completing the book *11 Months in Treblinka: A Story Never Told*. After raising her two sons in Woodbury, Connecticut, Sharon now lives in Westport with her husband Paul.

Dana J. Graef

Dana J. Graef is an environmental anthropologist and creative writer. She has published articles and essays on mining, wildness, and climate change. Her work has appeared in *Rust + Moth*, *Split Rock Review*, *SAPIENS*, and elsewhere. She lives between the rivers and ridges of central Connecticut. Find her at www.danagraef.com.

Jeannine Graf

Jeannine Graf began her career as a marketing copywriter before transitioning into the world of narrative storytelling. Balancing her roles as a staff writer and copy editor for Fairfield University Magazine, she is one semester away from earning her MFA in Creative Writing at Fairfield. With a focus on creative nonfiction and a beloved family of interesting characters to write about, Jeannine's essays invite readers to embark on thought-provoking journeys that resonate long after the final sentence. A resident of Fairfield for the past 25 years, she is proud to be a part of this anthology of Connecticut writers.

Elizabeth Hilts

Elizabeth Hilts is the author of the *Inner Bitch* series of humorous self-help books (Sourcebooks/Hysteria). She lives and writes in a smallish Connecticut city.

Mackenzie Hurlbert

Mackenzie Hurlbert is a horror writer with publications in *Pyre*, *The 2021 CT Literary Anthology*, *Not One of Us*, and anthologies by *Flame Tree Press*, *Eerie River Publishing*, *October Nights Press*, and others. Mackenzie studied English and journalism at Southern Connecticut State University, attended WCSU's Dublin Writing Residency, and was a participant of the 2023 Futurescapes Writers Workshop. When she's not writing or traipsing through the local bookstore, she enjoys getting lost in the woods with her husband Paul and their dog Solo.

Vesna Jaksic Lowe

Vesna Jaksic Lowe is a writer, nonprofit communications consultant, and creator of the Immigrant Strong newsletter. Vesna, who grew up in the former Yugoslavia, has written about her immigrant experience for the *Connecticut Literary Anthology 2023* (Woodhall Press), *The New York Times*, *the Washington Post*, *Pigeon Pages*, *Catapult*, and the *New York Daily News*. She has an essay forthcoming in the *Back Where I Came From* anthology (Book*hug press, 2024). She participated in Tin House workshops in 2024 and 2021 and was the parent-fellow at the 2021 Martha's Vineyard Institute of Creative Writing conference.

B. Fulton Jennes

B. Fulton Jennes is an award-winning poet whose work has appeared widely in literary journals and anthologies. In 2022, Jennes' poem *Glyphs of a Gentle Going* won the Lascaux Prize; another poem, *Father to Son*, won the 2023 New Millennium Award. Her collection *Blinded Birds* (Finishing Line Press) received the 2022 International Book Award for a poetry chapbook. *FLOWN*—an elegy-in-verse to her late sister—will be published by *Porkbelly Press* in 2024. Jennes is poet laureate emerita of Ridgefield, CT. She hosts many workshops and readings, both online and in person, including the Poetry in the Garden summer series at Keeler Tavern Museum.

Mary Keating

Mary Keating is a poet and lawyer. She's the Poetry Editor for *ScribesMICRO*, a three-time Pushcart nominee, and runs her own law firm in Darien, CT. Her writing appears in several journals, including *Wordgathering*, *Poetry for the Ukraine*, and *SFWP*. She loves to share her work at open mics. Disabled for over fifty years, Mary served as Chairperson for Connecticut State Rehabilitation Council and Vice President of the Rowayton Library. She lives with her husband, Danny, in CT.

Sam Keller
Sam is a fiction writer and editor currently querying for an agent. Her short fiction has been published in *Narrative*, *Permafrost*, and *Cagibi*, among others. She grew up in South Africa and after a decade in London, moved with her family to Connecticut where she completed her MFA at Fairfield University. Her first novel, *The Light Remains*, was a finalist for the Fairfield Book Prize in 2021. Sam is busy working on her second novel.

Elisabeth Kennedy
Elisabeth Kennedy is a Connecticut-based poet and writer, who was born and raised in the Sunshine State. She has a BA in Communications from Emerson College, an MA in Applied Linguistics from Hunter College, and is currently pursuing her MFA in Poetry at Southern Connecticut State University. In addition to fast pens, Elisabeth enjoys exuberant singing, crossing cultures, and spending time in nature observing birds and the changing seasons. A Human Resources professional by day, she is lucky to have family and friends who understand the solitude of her writing life.

Frederick-Douglass Knowles II
Frederick-Douglass Knowles II is a Professor of English at Connecticut State Community College (Three Rivers Campus). He is an Emeritus Poet Laureate of Hartford, CT. Knowles has been the recipient of the Nutmeg Poetry Award and the Connecticut of The Arts Fellow in Artist Excellence for Poetry/ Creative Non-Fiction. He is a two-time Pushcart Prize nominee and the author of *BlackRoseCity*.

Ginny Lowe Connors

Ginny Lowe Connors is the author of five poetry collections; the most recent of which is *Without Goodbyes: From Puritan Deerfield to Mohawk Kahnawake* (Turning Point, 2021). Among her awards are the Sunken Garden Poetry Prize, Atlanta Review's Grand Prize, and the Founders Award, sponsored by the National Federation of State Poetry Societies. In 2018 she was named the winner of *Passager*'s annual Poetry Contest. In 2023 she was writer in residence at Trail Wood, former home of naturalist Edwin Way Teale. She holds an MFA in poetry from Vermont College of Fine Arts. As publisher of her own press, *Grayson Books*, Connors has edited a number of poetry anthologies, including *Forgotten Women: A Tribute in Poetry*. A Board Member of the Connecticut Poetry Society, she is co-editor of *Connecticut River Review*.

Nancy Manning

I hold an MFA in Poetry from Southern Connecticut State University. My work has appeared in an eclectic mix of publications, most recently *Humans of the World*, *Sad Girl Diaries*, *Noctua Review* and *Unmagnolia*. My poetry collections are entitled *Amethyst Garden*, *The Unspoken of Our Days*, and *What Glues Us Together*; my novel *Undertow of Silence* won the TAG publishing award. I teach high school English classes.

Moriah Maresh

Moriah wrote her first story when she was seven years old and hasn't stopped. She is an Assistant Professor of English at Goodwin University and holds a bachelor's in English from The Ohio State University, a master's in English from Central Connecticut State University, an MFA in Creative Writing from Fairfield University, and TEFL certification. Her creative nonfiction was first published in *Helix*

Literary Magazine. Currently, she is working on a new collection of creative nonfiction essays as well as a fantasy novel.

Dana McSwain

Dana McSwain is the author of the Gothic genre-bender *Roseneath* (2020), winner of four national independent press awards. Her previous books include *Winter's Gambit* and *Winter's Roulette*, the cult-favorite action-adventure series set in the Rust Belt. Her work has been published in *Belt Magazine*, *The Atherton Review*, *Literary Cleveland*, *Scene Magazine*, and *Medium*. Her chilling short story, *Bus Stop*, was included in Akashic Book's Cleveland *Noir Anthology* (2023). Her newest title, *Relict*, the much-anticipated sequel to *Roseneath*, will be released in 2024 by Webb House Publishing. She lives in Connecticut with her family and two benevolent standard poodles.

Pat Mottola

Pat Mottola teaches Creative Writing at Southern Connecticut State University, where she earned both an M.S. in Art Education and an M.F.A. in Creative Writing. In addition to working with students at S.C.S.U., she is thrilled to teach both art and poetry to senior citizens throughout Connecticut. An award-winning poet and Pushcart Prize nominee, her work is published in journals across the country, including *War, Literature & the Arts*, *Connecticut Review*, *Main Street Rag*, *San Pedro River Review*, *VietNow Magazine*, and *Paterson Literary Review*. Pat is President of the Connecticut Poetry Society. She served as editor of *Connecticut River Review* from 2012–2017. On a global scale, she mentors Afghan women writers living in Afghanistan and beyond. Their recent poetry collection, *Maybe I Should Fly*, is published by Grayson Books. She is the author of two collections of poetry, *Under the Red Dress* (Five Oaks Press) and *After Hours* (Five Oaks Press). Her third book is forthcoming from Grayson Books. Pat was the recipient of the prestigious CSCU system-wide Board of

Regents Outstanding Teacher Award in 2019, as well as the J. Philip Smith Outstanding Teacher Award in 2021. She is the Poet Laureate of Cheshire, CT.

Steven Ostrowski

Steven Ostrowski is a widely published poet, fiction writer, painter, and songwriter. His novel, *The Highway of Spirit and Bone*, was published in 2023 by Lefora Publications and has been called "...a literary road trip for the ages." His poetry chapbook, *Persons of Interest*, won the 2021 Wolfson Chapbook Prize and was published in 2022. Steven and his son Ben coauthored a full-length collaboration called *Penultimate Human Constellation*, published in 2018 by Tolsun Books. Steven's newest book of poems, *Life Field*, (Impspired Press, UK) was published in March of 2024. His paintings have been published in *Lily Poetry Review, William and Mary Review, Stone Boat, Another Chicago Magazine*, and many other literary journals. He is Professor Emeritus at Central Connecticut State University. You can view and order copies of his work at www.stevenostrowski.org.

Jen Payne

Jen Payne is inspired by those life moments that move us most—love and loss, joy and disappointment, milestones and turning points. When she is not exploring our connections with one another, she enjoys contemplating our relationships with nature, creativity, and spirituality. Jen has published four books: *Look Up! Musings on the Nature of Mindfulness; Evidence of Flossing: What We Leave Behind; Waiting Out the Storm;* and *Water Under the Bridge: A Sort-of Love Story*. Her new book of poetry, *Sleeping with Ghosts*, will be published in the fall of 2024. Her work has appeared in numerous publications including the national anthology *Coffee Poems: Reflections on Life with Coffee* and the *Guilford Poets Guild 20th Anniversary Anthology*, in *The Perch*, a publication by the Yale Program for Recovery & Community

Health, and in *Waking Up to the Earth: Connecticut Poets in a Time of Global Climate Crisis*, edited by Connecticut's then Poet Laureate Margaret Gibson, funded by the Academy of American Poets. She writes regularly at randomactsofwriting.net.

Jess Rawling

Jess Rawling is a poet, interdisciplinary artist, educator, and life-long CT Valley Girl. She holds a BA from UMass and an MFA from SCSU and teaches Writing Seminars at Sacred Heart University when she isn't buying art supplies she doesn't need, starring in seedy puppet films, or playing gigs with her ukulele. Jess recently completed an artist residency on Martha's Vineyard, is a recipient of a 2023 Artist Fellowship Grant with support from the Connecticut Office of the Arts, which also receives funding from the National Endowment for the Arts, a federal agency, and is working on a folk opera and her first book of poetry. Her work has been published in a "Beyond Queer Words International Anthology" by *Beyond Words Literary Magazine*, by the online journal *Twin Pies Literary*, and by the collaborative online journal *Icebreakers Lit*; the latter piece was nominated for the 2024 Best of the Net Awards through *Sundress Publications*.

Joan Riordan

Joan Riordan is an educator with decades of experience. She enjoys writing, baking, and taking long walks. Fall is her favorite season and caramel apples are a favorite fall treat. You can see more of her poetry in print in *Things We Eat*, *What is a Friend?*, *What is a Family?*, *Autumnatopoeia* (Little Thoughts Press); and *Food* (The Toy Press) and online in the *Dirigible Balloon* and *Tyger Tyger* magazine.

Jillian Ross

Jillian Ross is a writer and garden designer who has taught Fiction I Workshop at Fairfield University. She finds writing—like teaching and design—to be a combination of art and craft, enhanced by a dose of inspiration. She strives to combine these elements in all of her work and keep the weeds under control. Jillian earned her MFA in Creative Writing at Fairfield University in 2013. Her work has appeared in *Dappled Things, The Noctua Review, r.kv.r.y., Dogwood, The Penwood Review, Extracts, Poetry Quarterly, Mason's Road, Weston Magazine, The Country Capitalist, Fairfield County Life*, and *Connecticut Gardener*. Jillian lives in Connecticut with two rescue cats—CopyCat, and, of course, FelixCityKitty who is featured in this work.

Katherine E. Schneider

Katherine E. Schneider is a poet living in Norwalk, CT. She holds an MFA from Fairfield University's MFA program where she worked closely with Baron Wormser and Dr. Kim Bridgford. She has also obtained an MA in TESOL and taught adult ESL in the greater NYC area for 10 years before obtaining a third master's degree in data science. Being an active participant in creative community is important to her. Katherine co-founded and co-hosts the online literary livestream FUMFA Poets & Writers Live with her MFA colleague and friend, fiction writer Chris Belden, with whom she also organizes monthly in-person open mics at Eco Evolution. Katherine enjoys combining poetry with music and other creative arts as well. Her endeavors in this regard can be followed on social media at @the_story_of_how. Her first chapbook, *I Used to Remember the Story of How*, was published by Finishing Line Press in 2019. Her publication credits for individual poems include *Ruminate, Blue Line, The Poetry Porch, The Paddock Review, Collateral*, and the *2023 Connecticut Literary Anthology*. Katherine's poem *Breath* was a nominee for a Pushcart Prize, and her latest manuscript, *Breaking the Fever*, was a finalist for the Fairfield Book Prize.

Natalie Schriefer

Natalie Schriefer, MFA is a bi/demi writer often grappling with sexuality, identity, and shame. She loves asking people about their fictional crushes (her most recent are Riza Hawkeye and Gamora). A Best of the Net nominee, her work has appeared online with *CNN*, *Wired*, *Insider*, and *NBC*, among others. Find her on Twitter @schriefern1 or on her website at www.natalieschriefer.com.

Jeff Schwartz

Jeff Schwartz grew up in Ohio and lives in Connecticut, where he has taught for the last 35 years. He was an early member of Alice James Books and has poems recently in the *Berru Poetry Series*, *Pedestal*, *Hanging Loose*, and *Naugatuck River Review*. He also writes frequently on student-centered learning.

Jack Sheedy

Jack Sheedy's chapbook *The Wanting Place* was published in 2021. His poetry has also appeared in several anthologies, including *BEAT-itude: National Beat Poetry Festival 10 Year Anthology; Poets to Come: A Poetry Anthology Celebrating Walt Whitman's Bicentennial*; and *Mad River Anthology 2018* and *2019*. He is the author of *Guardrail Nikes*, a winner in the Warner Theatre's Connecticut One-Act Play Festival in Torrington, Connecticut, in 2000. His play *Moratorium* was produced as a virtual reading by Pittsburgh New Works Festival in 2021. His memoir, *Sting of the Heat Bug* was published by Signalman Publishing in 2012. In 2020, he published *Magical Acts in Two Suitcases*, a collection of essays. As a journalist, he has won awards from the Society of Professional Journalists-CT Chapter and the New England Newspaper and Press Association. He is a former news editor for *The Catholic Transcript*, the magazine of the *Archdiocese of Hartford*, and is a features correspondent for the *Register Citizen*.

Sheedy is a member of OWL Poets, the Connecticut Poetry Society, and the Authors Guild. He lives in Harwinton, CT.

David Sheskin

David Sheskin is a former university professor and the author of *The Handbook of Parametric and Nonparametric Statistical Procedures* (Chapman and Hall). A writer of fiction and an artist, his work has been published extensively over the years. Most recently he has appeared in *The Los Angeles Review, The Journal of Humanistic Mathematics, The Font, The Dalhousie Review* and *Cleaver Magazine*. His most recent books are *Art That Speaks, David Sheskin's Cabinet of Curiosities,* and *Outrageous Wedding Announcements*.

Heidi St. Jean

Heidi St. Jean received her Master of Fine Arts in Creative Writing/ Poetry from Fairfield University, where she was selected as the sole recipient of its 2013 Academic Achievement Award for the MFA Program. She is a prize-winning poet and award-winning creative writer. Her poetry and essays continue to be published in numerous literary journals and anthologies. She also has served as managing editor and poetry editor for multiple journals. Her ekphrastic collaborations have also appeared in several museum exhibitions throughout the Northeast. She works professionally as a creative strategist, thought leadership writer, and editor.

Tim Stobierski

Tim Stobierski writes about relationships. His work explores themes of love, lust, longing, and loss — presented through the lens of his own experiences as a queer man. His poetry has been published in a number of journals, including the *Connecticut River Review, Gay & Lesbian Review,* and *Midwest Quarterly*. His first book of poems, *Dancehall,* was published by Antrim House Books in July 2023. An earlier chapbook, *Chronicles of a Bee Whisperer*, was published by River Otter Press in 2012.

Linda Strange

I am a writer and teacher of English as a Second Language in a public school in Waterbury, Connecticut. My essays about Ukrainian and Russian current events have appeared in *Pangyrus*, and my short fiction has appeared or is forthcoming in *Freshwater Literary Journal*, *Glass Mountain*, and *Marrow Magazine*. I live in Southbury between two streams with my English husband and a silver Himalayan called Quince.

Mary Vallo

Mary Vallo is a writer, former magazine editor and writing instructor who lives in New Milford, CT. Her essays and poetry have been included in anthologies and literary magazines and her children's book *How to Spend A Snowy Morning* is available on Amazon.

Tiffany Washington

Tiffany Washington is a high school English teacher, mother of four, lesbian, poet, and writer. Her works have appeared in a number of print and on-line publications including *Long River Run*, *Thimble Magazine*, *Sheila-Na-Gig* and most recently *Torrid Literature Journal*.

Laura Taylor White

Laura White grew up in a Navy family, crisscrossing the country every couple years. Big moves are kind of her thing, but she has put down roots in Old Greenwich, Connecticut with her husband to raise their two daughters. She studied English and Theater at Davidson College and is now an MFA candidate in Dramatic Writing at Fairfield University. Chances are, right now Laura is at her desk writing stories too big for this world, driving her daughters to dance or walking her two slobbery dogs.

A.H. Williams

A.H. Williams is a fiction writer from Norwalk, CT. In 2017, he graduated from Western Connecticut State University with a degree in accounting. Afterwards, he enlisted in the Navy as an Aviation Support Equipment Technician. During his 4-year contract he was stationed at FRCSW Det Pt. Mugu, and on board the USS Wasp. He is currently pursuing his MFA in Creative Writing at Fairfield University and hopes to make a name for himself in the world of fiction.

About the Editors

Rachel Baila

Rachel Baila is a writer and holistic-healing practitioner based in beautiful East Tennessee. Her poetry, articles, and travel-writing have been published in numerous journals, but her soft spot is with *Fauxmoir*, where she serves as chief editor. She has a Master of Arts in Teaching, further education in literacy studies, and is working toward an MFA in Creative Writing.

Victoria Buitron

Victoria Buitron is an award-winning writer and creative writing instructor who hails from Ecuador and resides in Connecticut. She received an MFA in Creative Writing from Fairfield University. She is currently the Competitions Editor for *Harbor Review*. Her work has appeared in *The Normal School, Shenandoah, The Acentos Review*, and *HuffPost*, among others. Her debut memoir-in-essays, *A Body Across Two Hemispheres*, was the 2021 Fairfield Book Prize winner. Her flash fiction was selected for 2022's *Best Small Fictions* and *Wigleaf's Top 50*. In 2023, she received the *Artistic Excellence Award* from the Connecticut Office of the Arts, which also receives funding from the National Endowment for the Arts. *Craigardan, Tin House, GrubStreet, Sundress Publications* and more organizations have championed her work through grants or writing residencies. Because she embraces creative chaos, she is also working on a novel about love, violence, and betrayal.

Christine Kandic Torres

Christine Kandic Torres is the author of the novel, *The Girls in Queens* (HarperVia, 2022), which was selected for the American Library Association's 2023 Rise Feminist Booklist. Her Pushcart Prize-nominated short fiction has been published in outlets such as *The Offing, Wigleaf, Fractured Lit,* and *Kweli,* while her nonfiction work has appeared in *Literary Hub* and *Electric Literature.* A Hedgebrook, VONA, and Vermont Studio Center alum, she is also the recipient of a Jerome Foundation emerging artist fellowship for fiction at the Anderson Center, and a New Work Grant from the Queens Council on the Arts. She currently lives in Fairfield, CT, where she is at work on her second novel.

Christopher Madden

Series Editor Christopher Madden is a writer, educator, and founder of Woodhall Press where he serves as the executive editor. He has a BA in English Literature from the University of Wisconsin, and an MFA in Fiction Writing from Fairfield University and an MFA in creative writing from Fairfield University. He is co-director of Bridgeport's Black Rock Arts Guild performing artists. He has edited numerous books including *Catchlight,* a Kirkus Best Book of 2020; *The Astronaut's Son,* a Foreword Indies winner for thriller/mystery; and *Light on Bone,* winner of the 2023 Maine Writers and Publishers Alliance literary award for crime fiction.

Summer Tate

Summer Tate is an educator and poet that has published poetry in *Meat for Tea: The Valley Review, Here Poetry Journal,* Eastern Connecticut State University and *Connecticut Literary Anthology,* Woodhall Press. She teaches English to high schoolers in Hartford, Connecticut and has been an adjunct professor at Springfield College, Fairfield University and in the Second Chance Pell Program with

Asnuntuck College. Summer holds a BA from Bay Path University, a Master's in English Education from UConn and received her MFA in Creative Writing and Publishing from Fairfield University. She is currently pursuing for her PhD in English with a focus on Africana studies and Anthropology. Summer Tate currently resides with her children in Windsor, Connecticut.